D0926241

PULL
OVER,
PLEASE

What To Do When the Police Stop You

PULL OVER, PLEASE

Brian Lawrie and Ian McLean

1985
Doubleday Canada Limited, Toronto, Ontario
Doubleday and Company, Inc., Garden City, New York

Library of Congress Catalog Card Number 85-10204

Copyright © 1985 by Brian Lawrie and Ian McLean

All rights reserved.
First edition.

Typeset by Compeer Typographical Services Limited
Printed and bound in Canada by Tri-Graphic Printing
   (Ottawa) Limited
Design by Donald Fernley

Canadian Cataloguing in Publication Data

Lawrie, Brian.
   Pull over please

Includes index.
ISBN 0-385-23145-8

1. Traffic violations — Canada.   2. Liability
for traffic accidents — Canada.   3. Highway law
— Canada.   I. McLean, Ian.   II. Title.

KE2114.L38 1985   345.71'0247   C85-098318-5

Contents

PULL
OVER,
PLEASE

Introduction

You have just received what is perhaps your first traffic ticket. You may take some comfort from the knowledge that your situation is not unique. Across Canada, millions of tickets are issued each year. Yet many people don't know what to do when they receive a ticket, or what consequences result from being found guilty of the offence with which they are charged.

Our experience demonstrates that people are very concerned about demerit points. What will be the impact of a conviction on their licence? For many people, losing their licence means the very loss of their livelihood. Travelling salesmen, taxi drivers, and truckers, to name three obvious examples, need licences to earn their livings.

People are also very concerned about how their insurance rates may be affected by a conviction. When your insurance company learns that you have been convicted of careless driving, your premiums for the next three years will at least double. There is more at stake in being found guilty of a traffic offence than the value of the ticket.

And yet, with so much at stake, people continue to go into court to challenge their tickets unprepared and unaware of what faces them. The court is not a place where one feels comfortable, and its procedures are unsettling and foreign. At the same time, it is the place where you must present your case, and it is essential that you be prepared and aware.

The purpose of this book is to help you understand your rights and responsibilities and to help you through the course to follow in responding to your ticket. Remember, in traffic ticket cases, you are not a criminal and you won't be treated like one. You won't be thrown in jail, and you won't be dragged through the criminal courts in handcuffs.

The process you will go through, however, will require considered choices and this book will help you make those choices. Every choice you make results in certain consequences and these should be kept in mind as you make each decision.

You can find yourself involved in criminal proceedings, however, as a driver. Drinking and driving offences are considered criminal in nature, as is dangerous driving and "failure to remain." For completeness, we have included a chapter which covers the consequences of these offences.

As soon as you receive a ticket, immediate questions come to mind. What do I do now? What happens if I am convicted? Can I lose my licence? Will my insurance rates be prejudiced? Our experience indicates that people worry unnecessarily about their tickets. Much of this worry could be avoided if they understood the process.

Many charges can be laid relating to motor vehicles. From failure to drive with your seat belt fastened to careless driving. Failure to remain at the scene of an accident, failing to stop at a stop sign, making an unsafe lane change, and failing to yield the right-of-way all result in different consequences. In all of these cases, however, the same process will be followed in the courts.

It should be noted that this book is also of value in understanding how the court system works in matters not related to motor vehicles. If you are charged with a liquor offence, a water pollution offence, a by-law infraction, or a hunting offence, the same procedures will apply. The information in this book can be applied to any offence as far as its discussion of court procedure and evidence. To indicate how sections can be used in other than a traffic context, we have included examples of court procedure in relation to other offences.

Pull Over, Please will guide you through the process of dealing effectively with your ticket. The book is divided into concise chapters dealing with procedures, your rights, your options, the trial process, how to conduct your case effectively, and the consequences of a conviction.

Pull Over, Please is a handbook for the layperson. We make as few assumptions as possible and try to answer questions which commonly arise at each stage of the process. Some questions we can't answer, including those relating to costs. Obviously, if you are going to conduct your case, your direct costs are reduced. If you retain an agent, your costs are increased, but less so than if you retain a lawyer. It goes without saying that if you lose time from work in the preparation and presentation of your case, this will be another cost to you.

Though driving offences, as opposed to criminal offences, are considered of a minor nature, they are what bring most people into contact with the judicial system. And, with few exceptions, the court assumes the defendant understands its process. In actual fact, the layperson may very well be ignorant, and this means that he or she may become overwhelmed by the court's formality and intimidated into making poor decisions. We are convinced that if you are better informed, if you understand your rights and the process in which you are involved, everyone gains. A police officer takes no pride in a sloppy performance that results in a conviction — he has an interest in justice being done in an appropriate and efficient manner.

We will discuss in detail the behaviour of the motorist at the scene of an accident. Inevitably, if two cars have collided, charges will be laid. We will show how you can present your position to your best advantage, and how you can negotiate at each step along the way. It is often possible to negotiate a lesser charge.

Of course, the best advice we can give our readers is to do everything possible to avoid becoming involved in the process. Driving defensively and keeping your car in good working order can help you avoid the problems that this book intends to help you solve. Having said that, however, we recognize such involvement is not a matter necessarily within one's control.

Pull Over, Please is not meant to be a legal textbook. It is a guide, a tool to assist you through a process with which you may not be familiar. The prosecution by the state is handled by professionals, a trained prosecutor and trained, professional police witnesses. The use of this book will help you present your own case clearly and effectively and assist you in making informed decisions. We have tried to make this book universally applicable, but there will be slight variations from province to province with regard to specific offences and penalties. Take some time to research your provincial law and use that information to supplement the information provided here.

Remember, a ticket does not go away. The state has inexhaustible time and resources to prosecute you. You must deal with it. It is our hope that this book will help.

1
Getting a Traffic Ticket

When You're Stopped

There is no adequate description of that feeling, deep in the pit of your stomach, when you realize that those red lights in the rearview mirror are flashing just for *you* or that the accusing finger from the uniformed man on the highway is pointed right at *you*. But these are the realities of modern-day driving.

Time seems to slow down as you wait for the approach of the police officer. Your blood pressure rises, as does your level of adrenalin, and you ask yourself "What did I do?" The initial conversation is usually cordial. "Good day. May I see your driver's licence, ownership, and insurance please?" Still you haven't got the answer to your question. A police officer may, of course, stop any vehicle on a highway to check that the driver is licenced. You don't have to commit an offence to be stopped. This scenario is repeated, across Canada, thousands of times every day. You, as a motorist, should understand and appreciate the importance of this initial contact. A police officer is what is termed, "an independent Agent of the Crown." This means that he is allowed to exercise discretion when dealing with offenders — he can issue a ticket, or just a caution, as he sees fit.

This initial stage is crucial if you wish to avoid a long, drawn out, legal process. Now is the time to make your explana-

1

tion of what led up to the alleged violation, whether it was speeding, running a red light, or driving without the proper authorization. Remain calm, take a deep breath, and attempt to explain yourself in a rational and truthful manner. If you are irritated, control your feelings. Remember, a police officer is human. He responds to common courtesy much the same way as any one. He is, however, also a trained observer and investigator. Therefore, you should take pains to be polite and honest. You don't have to grovel, but by the same token you should not be overly aggressive. Reason should prevail. Make your point in a reasonable manner and it will have the best effect.

James P. was stopped after meeting a police car on a one-way street. He explained he had just turned onto the street and he hadn't seen any signs. He saw the look of disbelief on the officer's face, but instead of entering into a fruitless argument, he used the time as the officer wrote out the ticket, to walk back to the intersection from which he had just turned. A large furniture truck was parked there, obscuring the warning signs. When he pointed this out to the officer, apologies were exchanged and the ticket cancelled.

If the police officer remains unimpressed by your explanation, and issues a ticket anyway, be aware that the ticket does not mean you are guilty. What it does, in effect, is move the arena of debate from the side of the highway to a courtroom. It also introduces an independent and impartial third party — a judge, or justice of the peace — who will listen to the facts of the case, and then reach a decision.

However inconvenient or unfair this may seem to you, resist the temptation to vent your anger on the police officer. He deals with many motorists during the course of a day, and he hears the same explanations and excuses from the guilty as well as from the innocent. In most cases he is unable to distinguish who is telling the truth. Your outburst won't help him — or you.

Make sure that you understand what you have been charged

with, and, if possible, immediately return to the "scene of the crime." Make note of road signs, road conditions, volume of traffic, lighting conditions, the officer's line of sight, any apparent obstructions, and other factors which you feel may help your defence.

The Traffic Ticket

The ticket you have received is an official document, your formal notification that the crown, in the person of the police officer, intends to institute legal proceedings against you and to prosecute you, in court, for the alleged offence described on the face of the ticket. This is the substance of what you will read when you turn the ticket over and examine the fine print. That may sound ominous and your first impulse may be to chuck the ticket into your deepest drawer. Don't. In order to handle this ticket effectively, you need all the information you can get. Reading the ticket carefully is the first step.

When you are presented with a ticket you may receive, as well, a separate explanatory notice — read this carefully also. It contains all the information you need to respond to the ticket. It is important that you act within the prescribed time limits on the ticket. Ignoring it will result in a financial snowballing that could even lead to your arrest. The ticket itself is completed by the police officer in a prescribed and regulated manner. Examples of tickets appear on pages 4 and 5, for comparison with your own.

There is a popular misconception that the slightest mistake on the ticket will result in the case being dismissed. In fact, there are only five areas in which an error may result in a dismissal. These are: the date of the offence; the citation of your name; the location of the offence; the details of the offence; and the time and date for your appearance in court.

These points on the ticket should always be checked thor-

OFFENCE NOTICE

FORM 102.
THE PROVINCIAL
OFFENCES ACT. 1979

PROVINCIAL
OFFENCES COURTS
PROVINCE OF ONTARIO

87063

YOU ARE CHARGED WITH THE FOLLOWING OFFENCE:

On the **9** day of **NOVEMBER** 19 **84** Time **10.25** | A / M |

NAME **JONES   STEVEN   S.**

ADDRESS **67, ST. CLAIR AVE. W.**

TORONTO , ONTARIO M2M 3G6

DRIVER'S LICENCE NO:			CLASS	COND.
J0323	71145	20616	G	NIL

	BIRTH DATE		REGISTRATION NO.	YEAR	PROVINCE	MAKE
SEX	DAY	MO.	YEAR				
M	16	06	52	SEG 097	85	ONTARIO	CHEN

AT **SOUTHBOUND WINONA DRIVE**
AT VAUGHAN RD.   YORK

DID COMMIT THE OFFENCE OF **DISOBEY**
STOP SIGN — FAIL TO
STOP

CONTRARY TO **HIGHWAY TRAFFIC ACT**

SECTION

116 (a)

NOTICE

WITHIN 15 DAYS OF RECEIVING THIS OFFENCE NOTICE YOU MAY CHOOSE ONE OF THE OPTIONS ON THE BACK OF THIS FORM. IF YOU DO NOTHING A CONVICTION SHALL BE ENTERED AGAINST YOU, AND FINE PAYMENT ENFORCEMENT WILL FOLLOW.

OFFICER NO	UNIT
5732	13

IF YOU PLEAD NOT GUILTY THE TRIAL SHALL BE HELD AT

2265 KEELE STREET, NORTH YORK

SET FINE (including costs)

$ 53 00

IF YOU WISH TO PAY THE SET FINE SHOWN, SIGN THE PLEA OF GUILTY ON THE BACK AND FORWARD YOUR PAYMENT AND THIS NOTICE TO THE ADDRESS OF THE COURT SHOWN ON THE BACK OF THIS NOTICE.

PROVINCIAL OFFENCES
OFFICERS ARE NOT
ALLOWED TO ACCEPT
PAYMENT OR DOCUMENTS
FOR DELIVERY TO
THE COURT.

V Smith

SIGNATURE OF ISSUING
PROVINCIAL OFFENCES OFFICER

Date of service if other than offence date

Day	Month	Year

4

FORM 101.
THE PROVINCIAL
OFFENCES ACT, 1979

CERTIFICATE OF OFFENCE

PROVINCIAL
OFFENCES COURTS
PROVINCE OF ONTARIO

87063

On the 9 day of NOVEMBER 19 84 Time 10:25 A M

NAME JONES STEVEN S.
(LAST) (FIRST) (MIDDLE)

ADDRESS 67 ST. CLAIR AVE. W.
(NUMBER AND STREET)

TORONTO ONTARIO M2M 3G6
(MUNICIPALITY) (P.O.) (PROVINCE) (POSTAL CODE)

DRIVER'S LICENCE NO.					CLASS	COND.
J 0 3 2 3	7 1 1 4 5	2 0 6 1 6			G	NIL

SEX	BIRTH DATE DAY MO. YEAR	REGISTRATION NO.	YEAR	PROVINCE	MAKE
M	16 06 52	SEG 097	85	ONTARIO	CHE V

AT SOUTHBOUND WINONA DRIVE
AT VAUGHAN RD. YORK.
(MUNICIPALITY)

87063

DID COMMIT THE OFFENCE OF DISOBEY
STOP SIGN — FAIL TO
STOP.

CONTRARY TO HIGHWAY TRAFFIC ACT
SECTION 116(a) .

I believe and certify the above offence has been committed and certify that I served an *offence notice* personally upon the person charged on the offence date

~Smith~

SIGNATURE OF PROVINCIAL OFFENCES OFFICER

I believe and certify the above offence has been committed and certify that I served a *summons* personally upon the person charged on the offence date

SIGNATURE OF PROVINCIAL OFFENCES OFFICER

OFFICER NO.	5732	UNIT	13

OFFICER NO.		UNIT	

Summons issued for

On the day of next at M

AT

courtroom

SET FINE (including costs) $ 53 00 XX	(Sec 3(4) Provincial Offences Act, 1979)	~S. Jones~ SIGNATURE OF PERSON CHARGED

CONVICTION ENTERED SET FINE IMPOSED (POA-SECTION 9a)		Address Code					Court Rm.
DATE DAY	MO. YEAR	M	U	C	B	Code	
		Day Crt. 1	2	Month		Day	
		3	4				
		Night Crt.					
JUSTICE		P.I. ☐	P.D. ☐				

5

oughly. A mistake in any one of them will not automatically result in a dismissal, but a strong argument can be made which may convince the court that your case has been prejudiced and that the charge should be dismissed.

Date of the Offence

The date of offence must be correct.

The time of offence should also be correct, but a motion by the prosecution to amend the time portion of the ticket is almost certain to be granted and the case will proceed.

Your Name

Your name on the ticket must appear in such a form as to sufficiently identify you as the person who is alleged to have committed the offence. A slight deviation from the correct spelling of your name may or may not be enough to result in a dismissal. This decision will rest with the justice of the peace or judge who hears your case, and will be based on arguments presented by each side.

Location of the Offence

The location of the offence is important when it comes to establishing the jurisdiction of the court.

Each court is empowered to hear cases only from within a specified area, known as the judicial district. If it can be shown that the location for the offence, as shown on the ticket, is not within the court's judicial district, then that court has no authority to hear the case. When an alleged offence takes place near the boundary of two judicial districts, check the location carefully.

It is also important that the municipality be included on the ticket, since it is usually this information which establishes jurisdiction. But an error of a few house numbers, or even a city block or two, is likely to be easily amended and will not affect the court's ability to hear the case.

Details of the Offence

The details of the offence should appear on the face of the ticket and be clear enough to allow you to understand the charge. Statute and section numbers must be included. This is to allow you to be able to properly research and defend yourself against the charge. You should also verify that the section number under which you are charged corresponds to the offence as it is described on the face of the ticket.

Government bookstores and libraries have copies of the statutes, so that you can investigate the charge.

Time and Date for Your Appearance

The time and date set for your appearance in court must be correct. From time to time scheduling mistakes occur. If you are told to appear, for example, at 3:00 A.M. it is an obvious error. Your case would probably come up in the 3:00 P.M. court. Should you not appear at 3:00 P.M., however, the court would have no power to proceed, since there would be no way of knowing if you had appeared at 3:00 A.M. The mistake would be the crown's and would have to be accepted as such. The case could be dismissed.

What Are Your Options?

Now that you understand the charge against you, you are faced with a decision. You have three basic options: pleading "guilty;" "guilty with an explanation;" or "not guilty."

The Plea of "Guilty"

Choose this option when there is no dispute over the facts, and you wish to conclude the matter by paying the fine shown on the face of the ticket. A court appearence is not necessary to exercise this option. Mail the ticket, with a cheque or money order, to the court indicated on the reverse of the ticket. Remember, it is your responsibility for the ticket and payment to reach the court within the required time. If, for any reason, it does not, you may be subject to additional fines. This option is generally irreversible, so make sure your decision is carefully considered.

The Plea of "Guilty with an Explanation"

This is the plea to choose when there is no dispute over the facts, but you want to inform the court of some circumstance which might alter the penalty; or you wish to extend the time period over which you pay the fine.

It is important to realize that this is still a guilty plea. A conviction will be registered and demerit points assessed. To exercise this option you must visit the courthouse and appear before a justice of the peace. This is normally conducted in an informal setting on a one-to-one basis.

Consider this option carefully and be sure that what you consider "an explanation" is not, in fact, a valid defence that might lead to an acquittal.

This is an example of a valid explanation: You receive news that your child is ill at school, and you drive over to pick him up. On the way, you are stopped by a police officer who monitored you on radar and gave you a ticket for speeding. Although the offence was committed, if you explain the circumstances to the justice of the peace — the fact that you were worried and distracted, and that before this your driving record was unblemished — then he may reduce or suspend the fine.

Here is an example of an "explanation" which is, in fact, a defence: A woman is involved in a serious accident. It is discovered that the car she is driving was not insured. Her husband, the registered owner, is charged with having no insurance. Taken at face value, it would appear simple enough; you either have insurance or don't. The husband enters a plea of guilty with an explanation.

He explains to the court that he owns two cars; one regularly used by his wife, and one which is used by him. He takes care of all of the documents relating to the cars and their maintenance. Recently he had become unemployed, and having no use for his vehicle, and to conserve money, he had the insurance cancelled. He didn't tell his wife because she never drove his car.

On the morning of the accident his wife was leaving for work and noticed that her car had a flat tire. She was late, so she decided to take her husband's car. Later she became involved in the accident.

Actually, this explanation is a defence of "honest mistake," and may very well have resulted in an acquittal. Unfortunately he pleaded guilty, was found guilty and fined $500.

The Plea of "Not Guilty"

When there is a dispute over the facts: You want to hear the evidence against you and put your own case forward—plead not guilty. To enter this plea you must notify the court of your intention, following the instructions on your ticket. Then you must attend court at the time appointed for your trial.

The not guilty plea will be discussed in greater detail in a moment, but first there is one more option to consider.

The Fourth Option

There is, of course, a fourth option: Ignoring it. Ignoring a ticket usually results in your automatic conviction at the end of fifteen days, or a period of time specified in your provincial legislation. Similarly, if you opt to plead not guilty but do not show up at the time appointed for your trial, a trial will be held in your absence (*ex parte*), and a conviction registered.

In both cases a fine is imposed. You will be notified by mail and instructed how and where to pay. If you continue to ignore it, your driver's licence may be suspended or a warrant may be issued for your arrest.

The bottom line? It is going to get more expensive and troublesome, not less. Deal with it and deal with it *promptly*. The consequences of ignoring a ticket are too severe to take chances on.

The Plea of "Not Guilty"

This option should be chosen not only when you know that you did not commit the offence, but also when you are not sure if you committed the offence.

For example: You are travelling on a highway and you see from your speedometer that your speed is 100 km/h. Some distance further on, a police officer stops you and says your speed was 120 km/h.

Although you're not aware of your exact speed as you entered the radar beam, you are convinced that you were still travelling at the 100 km/h speed limit.

You are entitled to go to court, plead not guilty, and have the prosecution *prove* that you were in fact speeding.

Pleading not guilty requires that the prosecutor prove, beyond a reasonable doubt, that the offence was committed and that it was committed by you. The advantage of the not guilty plea is that even if you can't remember if you disobeyed a sign or what speed you were going, you can compel the prosecutor to prove it — to you, as well as to the court.

10

This plea is mainly used however, when you have a defence to offer. Your defence should be prepared with the following watchwords uppermost in your mind: accuracy, brevity, and relevancy.

Accuracy

Accuracy is important. Measurements of distances, location of signs, time of day, and weather conditions *must* be accurate in order to convince the court and influence its decision. Words and phrases such as "about," "almost,"or "I think," should be avoided. Vagueness or doubt will damage your credibility.

With a little effort, most of the information you will require can be obtained from public records compiled and maintained by federal, provincial, and municipal transportation and environmental authorities. The addresses of departments whose records you feel may be of assistance to you can be found in the government section of your local telephone book. Always request certified copies of the required information. A small fee is usually charged for this service.

These public records will help to establish precise distances or road widths, weather conditions, or the duration of an amber light at a particular intersection. You can even find out how many accidents have occurred at a particular location over a given period of time.

Brevity

Brevity is important. Never use a sentence when a single word will suffice.

Here are some tips on how to be concise and effective. If you are asked a question by the court that can be answered yes or no, answer yes or no. Don't launch into a long-winded answer, it will only serve to confuse, frustrate, and bore the

11

court. Prepare your questions beforehand. Make them brief and to the point. Design them so that they produce only the point which you need to use in your argument (your final submission). If you want to prove that the weather conditions caused you to fail to stop, ask a direct question about the driving conditions that day. Don't ask for a general discussion of climate and how it relates to driving; keep to specifics. Make each submission to the point. Emphasize the arguments which support your position but don't repeat or re-hash them. You'll make a better impression by remaining businesslike. Traffic courts hear a tremendous number of cases; their time is precious.

Relevancy

Relevancy is important. Keep your explanations, arguments, and questions confined to what is relevant.

Examine the section under which you are charged carefully, prior to going to court. Pick out the points in that section which you wish to attack or deny. Make sure that you confine your case solely to these points. Irrelevant information or ill-considered statements or questions not only waste time, but can cause problems when the Rules of Evidence are applied. As a result, you could seriously damage your case.

The Rules of Evidence govern what evidence may be put before the court and also the manner in which it may be put before the court. Normally they prevent the prosecutor from introducing your previous driving record as evidence to support a guilty verdict on the present charge. However, if you are not careful and irrelevantly say something like "I am not guilty of speeding because I never speed" in your defence, you remove the prohibition on introducing previous convictions. You have unwittingly given what is known as "evidence of good character" and the prosecutor is entitled to bring up any previous convictions to rebut this. The fact that you never have exceeded the speed limit before is irrelevant in regard to your guilt or innocence on the speeding charge before the court. Although it is tempting to point out the good points of your driving record, be careful not to open avenues for potentially damaging evidence.

Take care to instruct your witnesses so that they too observe the accuracy, brevity, and relevancy watchwords.

Sidewalk Lawyers

One more piece of advice on making the decision of what to plea to the charge against you. Beware of sidewalk lawyers. This is a lesson that one young driver learned the hard way.

Tom V. pulled away from a stop sign onto Main Street. It was late at night and traffic was light. The cars ahead seemed perfectly spaced to allow him to wind his way in and out as he proceeded along. Never had he felt so good about his ability behind the wheel or the responsiveness of his car. Man and machine were in perfect harmony. The universe was unfolding as it should.

Suddenly, the poetic moment was shattered. In his rearview mirror appeared a dreaded flashing light, and the peace of the night was broken by an equally despised siren. At first, Tom thought the police were on a chase, but as he slowed to allow them room to pass the terrible truth dawned. If the police were involved in a chase, they had caught their prey.

The officer appeared at the window, demanding his license, ownership, and insurance documents. When he asked the officer to explain the problem, the answer was that the car had been clocked at 110 km/h in a 50 km/h zone.

This came as a complete shock to Tom. He realized he may have been going a little fast, maybe even in excess of the limit, but he had no idea he was going that fast. The officer appreciated his genuine surprise, and realizing the consequences of the offence for a young driver, he exercised his discretion in Tom's favor. He wrote up the ticket for speeding, stating that the car had been going 65 km/h in a 50 km/h zone. A trial date was also assigned.

The next day, the ticket came up in conversation. The sidewalk lawyers had what sounded like good advice to Tom. If the officer failed to show up in court, the case would be dismissed. Even if the officer did show up, how could he give proper evidence? Wouldn't he be in an untenable position? How could he give evidence that the offence was going 65 km/h, when the car had been going 110 km/h? He would be guilty of perjury! Wouldn't the court, unable to amend the ticket, have to dismiss the charge? Tom's other friends were less certain. They urged him to accept the officer's discretion and pay quietly. The question of guilt was not involved, surely it was better just to accept the penalty, rather than risk anything further.

The fight-at-all-costs side won. The appointed day arrived and all parties assembled in court. The case was called and up to the witness stand strode the officer. Taking the Bible in his right hand, he swore to tell the truth, the whole truth, and nothing but the truth. To Tom's great surprise, the evidence was as follows:

"I was working the 8:00 P.M. to 6:00 A.M. shift on routine patrol in a marked radar car. At 1:00 A.M. I observed a motor vehicle which I clocked at 110 km/h proceeding along Main Street in a westerly direction, weaving through traffic. I stopped the vehicle, spoke to the defendant and issued to him a ticket for speeding at 65 km/h. The defendant identified himself as . . .

It is not hard to imagine the surprise that Tom felt. Here he was pleading not guilty to a charge of which he knew he was guilty. Not only that, but the court was being told that it could have been far worse, if the officer hadn't decided to reduce the charge. Tom was too startled to make any cross-examination, and in his own defense admitted that he had

14

hoped the officer wouldn't show, or would feel he couldn't testify truthfully.

After a tongue-lashing from the judge, a heavy fine, and court costs into the bargain, the case came to its inglorious end. The moral of the story — beware of well-meaning but amateur advice.

2
Accidents

Procedure at the Scene of an Accident

Fortunately, the vast majority of motor vehicle accidents in Canada do not involve personal injury. They are property damage accidents, where the only casualties are sheet metal, glass, and pride.

Be that as it may, a motor vehicle accident is a traumatic experience for any driver. When the vehicles come to rest the trouble really begins. The very first thing to do is to make sure that no one is injured. When you are assured that nothing but perhaps a few nerves are shattered, make the scene safe by placing flares or having someone go down the road to warn approaching traffic. Never, never, assume that other drivers are aware of the traffic hazard. Be alert to the fact that you and the other persons involved in the accident are in an extremely vulnerable and dangerous situation. Too many minor accidents become fatal accidents when drivers and passengers get out on the highway, and, in their preoccupation, fail to realize the dangers.

The most important pieces of equipment you can carry in your car, in addition to your first-aid kit and fire extinguisher, are a pencil and paper. At the earliest opportunity get them and start writing. Write down the names and addresses of witnesses who may be standing nearby and the licence numbers of cars whose drivers and/or passengers may have seen

16

the accident. Licence numbers can be traced by police, and later they can find the owners' names and interview the potential witnesses.

Write down weather conditions, road conditions, traffic conditions, and *any* statements that other drivers or witnesses make. Note what happened before the accident: A cyclist made a suddent turn; the traffic lights had broken down; a stalled car blocked the inside lane; and any other relevant details. Sketch the scene. Jot down damages to the other vehicles, lighting conditions, and obstructions. If there are defects apparent on the other cars, such as faulty lights, make a note of them. Hold on to these notes.

In view of the shock involved after an accident you may find it extremely difficult to complete these notes. Force yourself, if you possibly can, to do so. You may want to put a paper clip on this chapter and keep this book in your glove compartment, so that you can refer to it right at the scene. Your notes can be invaluable if your case goes to civil or criminal court, or even for completing reports required by your insurance company.

Accident Report

If you become involved in a motor vehicle accident which involves personal injury or property damage in excess of a specified amount (which varies from province to province), you are required to give a report to the police, which is, in turn, passed on to the ministry of transportation.

The purpose of the report is to allow the government to assess whether or not changes or improvements to the roadway should be made to prevent similar accidents in the future. At least that is the intention of the legislation.

However, should you be charged with an offence resulting from that accident, you are likely to find the report and statement, which you gave in compliance with your statutory duty, entered into evidence at your trial. In order to prevent this, you must object to its future use at trial, at the time you make the statement.

In most cases, when you are asked for your account of what happened, you won't know whether the officer intends to lay a charge against you or not. You may also feel, however, that you have done nothing wrong and therefore you have nothing to hide. Beware: Once the spoken word becomes the written word, it is open to interpretation. You can unknowingly damage your case by a statement made under the emotional stress of an accident.

This can be avoided if, before you start into your formal statement of what occurred, you ask the officer to add the following clause to the beginning of your report:

> "I object to and claim privilege from the use of all, any part, or parts of this statement in any investigation or judicial proceedings whether criminal or civil. This statement is given solely for the information of the registrar of motor vehicles."

Demerit Points

Contrary to what many people may think, driving is a privilege, not a right, and the demerit point system was established to allow the ministries of transportation to maintain some form of supervision and control over drivers who may abuse that privilege.

The mechanics of the system are simple and vary little from province to province. Every driver starts with a clean record and no demerit points. The ministries have chosen the more serious driving offences and assigned a set number of demerit points to each of them. The exact number of demerit points attached to each specific offence is dependent on how serious it is. A complete list of offences and their demerit points appears on page 20. They range from

18

seven demerit points for failing to remain at the scene of an accident, to two demerit points for failing to lower your headlamp beams. The maximum number of accumulated demerit points is fifteen and at that point an automatic thirty-day licence suspension is imposed. Demerit points remain on your record for two years from the date of the offence, not the conviction. They are automatically assigned and cannot be reduced or altered by the court.

If you accumulate a total of nine demerit points, you may be required to visit a ministry office and explain why your licence should not be suspended immediately. You must also pledge to improve your driving habits. It is important to note that if you fail to satisfy the ministry official that you appreciate the seriousness of the situation, and that you plan to take steps to remedy the problem, you may have your licence suspended at this point.

In some provinces all new drivers must complete a period of probation and for these drivers the rules are different. These drivers are subject to suspension if they accumulate six demerit points during their probationary period. If the new driver probationary system applies in your province it will be explained to you when you receive your licence.

Accumulating demerit points has many negative effects on you as a driver. Not the least of which is the increase in insurance premiums that inevitably follows.

An interesting aspect of the demerit point system is that if you are convicted of an offence, such as disobeying a stop sign, while riding a bicycle, then demerit points will be assessed against your licence.

Demerit Point System

Points	Offences
7	Failing to remain at the scene of an accident
6	Careless driving; racing
	Failure to stop for a school bus
	Exceeding the speed limit by 50 km/h or more
5	Failure to stop for a school bus at an unprotected crossing
4	Exceeding the speed limit by 30-49 km/h
	Following too closely
3	Exceeding the speed limit by 16-29 km/h
	Driving through, around or under a railway crossing barrier
	Improper passing
	Crowding the driver's seat
	Wrong way on a one-way street or highway
	Failure to yield the right of way
	Failure to obey a stop sign, signal light, or railway crossing signal
	Failure to obey the directions of a police officer
	Failure to report an accident to the police
	Driving or operating a vehicle on a closed highway
	Improper driving where a highway is divided into lanes
2	Failure to share the road
	Failure to signal
	Failure to lower the headlamp beam
	Failure to obey signs other than those referred to above
	Pedestrian cross-over offence
	Improper or prohibited turns
	Unnecessary slow driving
	Improper opening of a vehicle door
	Towing persons on sleds, bicycles, skis, etc.
	Backing on highway

Car Insurance

An increasing number of provinces are adopting legislation requiring compulsory automobile insurance, and it is reasonable to assume that within the near future this legislation will be in place throughout Canada.

The need for adequate insurance coverage in the event of an accident is obvious and it should be considered a part of the cost of buying a car. What is not as obvious, however, is the effect poor driving habits have on your insurance premiums.

Insurance companies are profit-making institutions and as such take great pains to ensure that they do not become burdened with too many "liabilities." In the field of car insurance the "high-risk" driver, one who accumulates a high number of demerit points or is involved in an inordinate number of accidents, is a liability. Statistics show that this driver is more likely to cost the company money, and, as a result, they may offer very high insurance premiums.

In an effort to identify this person, insurance companies closely monitor the driving records of all their policy holders. When an insurance policy is due for renewal, the company will request a driving licence abstract from the ministry of transportation—not only for the automobile owner himself, but for everyone who regularly drives the insured car. These records are examined very closely. The total number of convictions are noted, and particular attention is paid to the types of offences committed.

Convictions under the Criminal Code of Canada in relation to motor vehicles, as well as some of the more serious offences under the provincial traffic laws have the greatest impact on your insurance premiums. These include:

- careless driving
- dangerous driving
- driving while licence is under suspension

- failure or refusal to submit to a breathalyzer test
- failure to pass a breathalyzer test
- failing to remain at the scene of an accident
- manslaughter or criminal negligence committed in the operation of a motor vehicle
- racing

A first conviction for any one of the foregoing offences brings about an automatic 50 percent increase in your premiums. A subsequent conviction for any one of these will result in a 100 percent increase. In actual practice, especially if an accident occurred at the same time, these increases can be substantially more. And conviction or accident related increases remain in effect as long as the accident or offence remains on your driving record. It is not difficult to see that an accident and a conviction for careless driving could cost a driver thousands of dollars over and above any fine imposed.

Here are a few more examples of convictions which will result in an increase in your insurance premiums.

A first conviction for failure to report an accident, failure to give required information at an accident, improper passing of school buses, or passing or speeding in school or playground zones will bring about a 15 percent increase in premiums. Any subsequent conviction allows for a further 5 percent increase.

Certain offences are viewed less seriously. These include:

- crowding the driver's seat
- crossing a railway barrier
- carrying a person in a trailer
- driving on the wrong side of road
- driving an unsafe vehicle
- driving unaccompanied by a licensed driver
- failure to have the proper trailer attachments
- failure to yield the right-of-way
- failure to share the road
- failure to stop as required

- failure to obey a traffic sign/control device
- following too closely
- impeding traffic
- improper passing
- improper use of, or failure to use, turn/stop signals
- making a prohibited U-turn
- pedestrian cross-over violations
- seat belt violations
- speeding
- stunting

No increase is levied for the first three convictions of these offences. A fourth conviction, however, brings about a 25 percent increase, and each subsequent conviction will result in a 15 percent increase.

Accidents involving an insured person are also considered when the policy is renewed. Although there is no surcharge for two accidents in the preceding three years, a third accident will bring about a 30 percent increase and each subsequent accident an additional 10 percent.

When a driver is faced with premium surcharges as a result of too many tickets or accidents there is, for some, a temptation to change insurance companies and not declare their actual driving record in order to get a lower premium. For those so inclined; a word of caution. False or misleading information on your application will probably result in the cancellation of your policy. Your insurance company, by virtue of the vast number of policies being processed, may not discover your misrepresentations immediately. Should you be unfortunate enough to be involved in a serious accident, however, and should the missing information come to light, it could result in your footing the entire bill for liability and repairs — a sobering thought.

Similarly, there may be a temptation to transfer ownership of your car to your brother or mother in order to benefit from their clean records and lower premiums. Again, it should be understood that if an investigation revealed that the person who ordinarily drove the car would, had all information been included, have been liable for a higher premium, the policy may be nullified.

The key fact to note as you consider the costs of insurance, is that if you concentrate your efforts on becoming a better driver, you can avoid all of these increases. No tickets and accidents means no unexpected premium increases.

Reciprocity

All of the provinces and a significant number of states in the U.S. are included in a reciprocity agreement regarding demerit points and drivers' licence suspensions.

Reciprocity means that if your driver's licence is suspended, or if you accumulate demerit points, in any of the provinces or states in the agreement, then the suspension will be enforced or the demerit points assessed wherever your driving record is held.

All ten provinces are involved in this agreement, as are the following states:

Alabama	Maryland	Oklahoma
Arizona	Michigan	Oregon
Arkansas	Minnesota	Pennsylvania
Colorado	Mississippi	Rhode Island
Connecticut	Missouri	South Carolina
Delaware	Montana	Tennessee
District of Columbia	Nebraska	Texas
Idaho	New Hampshire	Utah
Illinois	New Jersey	Virginia
Indiana	New Mexico	Washington
Iowa	New York	West Virginia
Kansas	North Carolina	Wisconsin
Kentucky	North Dakota	Wyoming
Louisiana	Ohio	

3
Speeding

The offence of speeding is one of the most common driving offences. And the supervision and control of motorists' speed on the country's highways has long been a high priority for safety experts and traffic enforcement officers.

To assist them, police departments use a variety of methods to detect and record speed. These range from a police car following, or pacing, a car suspected of speeding (as the officer uses his own speedometer to record the speed), through to the use of aircraft, and, of course, the dreaded radar.

The common denominator in all of these speed detection methods, and the most important factor from the point of view of the driver anxious to contest a speeding charge, is that the prosecuting officer has to rely on some form of mechanical device to back up his suspicion that the driver was speeding.

This is important for a defence against a speeding charge for two reasons. First, when giving evidence an officer must satisfy the court that he had reason to believe that the defendant was speeding, and that he then used a device to confirm this belief. For instance, it is not sufficient for him to say: "I was watching my radar set and saw a reading of 150 km/h come up on the display readout and the defendant's car was the only one on the road." The machine is only allowed to be used as a means to confirm what a police officer already suspected. Second, and perhaps most important, is that all speeding charges involve a mechanical device, and the functioning of any such device can be unreliable and inaccurate. The prosecution must prove, beyond a reasonable doubt, that the device used was accurate and an officer operating it was qualified.

The most common methods used for enforcing speed limits are outlined in this chapter, together with sample questions that may help you establish a defence argument.

Timed Measured Distance

In this procedure a stretch of roadway is pre-measured and marked, usually by white lines somewhere on the pavement at right angles to the flow of traffic. An observing officer then positions himself so he can see any two consecutive marks. He can do this by standing on higher ground or by using an aircraft.

When a car he suspects of speeding crosses one of these marks he starts a stopwatch, then, when the car crosses the next mark, he stops it. By referring to a time/distance table, he can determine the actual speed of the car. If the vehicle was in fact speeding, he will either stop the vehicle himself (if he is in a position to do so) or use his radio to identify the car for another officer, who will stop the car for him.

This procedure appears simple enough on the face of it. It is, however, potentially the most difficult for the prosecution to prove. As with any of these methods, if you want to fight your ticket, go through the procedure which was used to determine your speed step by step and look for any inaccuracies which may be present.

In court, ask the officer questions such as:

How do you know these marks were the stated distance apart? Did you measure the distance? Did you paint the marks?

How do you know the stopwatch was accurate? When was it tested? By whom? Is the tester present in court and willing to testify under oath on the accuracy of the stopwatch?

(If the tester is not, then the evidence of the stopwatch's accuracy becomes "hearsay" and as such should not be admitted [allowed]. The same applies, of course, to the painter of the roadway markings.)

Who prepared the time/distance table? Is that person present? Can he/she testify on the accuracy of the formula used to prepare the table?

When did you activate the stopwatch: When the front of the car crossed the mark, or was it the rear of the car?

When did you deactivate the stopwatch?

Pacing

If you were paced by a police car to determine your speed, the officer must not only prove the accuracy of his speedometer but also that you were followed in the prescribed manner. He must have been behind you and kept an equal distance between your vehicle and his. He must be able to say that there were no other vehicles between his car and yours and that he did not lose sight of your car at any time. He must also be able to say for what distance he followed you. The distance must have been sufficient to enable him to gain a fair and accurate determination of your speed.

If you contest a charge of speeding that was based on this method of evaluating your speed, ask:

What was the volume of traffic?
(Heavy volume decreases the accuracy and effectiveness of this method.)
What were the weather conditions?

Were you directly behind me? How far back were you?
For how long? For what distance?
(*Remember: Speed equals distance divided by time.*)
Did you lose sight of my vehicle at any time?
Has your speedometer been checked? When?
(*It must have been within a reasonable time before or after the alleged offence.*)
Who checked the speedometer? What method was used to do so?
(*If an officer did not check the speedometer himself, or if the method used involved a radar set operated by another officer, the other officer must also be in court to testify.*)

Some police forces have a card in the police vehicle that is updated whenever an officer checks the speedometer. The card itself does not constitute evidence as to when the speedometer was checked and how accurate it was.

Radar

Many thousands of motorists can attest to the effectiveness of this particular speed monitoring device, but not many know the reasons for its effectiveness or even the basic principles under which it functions.

The word itself describes its original purpose. Radio detection and ranging (radar) was developed and perfected during the Second World War. It was used to plot the location and course of enemy aircraft and allow more accurate interception. As with many technological advances made in wartime, it was very quickly adapted to peacetime use, much to the chagrin of the public.

The radar used by police works on a principle known as the Doppler theory of wave motion, which was discovered by an Austrian physicist named Christian Johann Doppler. A police radar functions on the principle that a radio wave striking an object and bouncing back undergoes a change in frequency and that the corresponding change in frequency is proportional to the speed of the object. In simple terms, radar can be explained using the following illustration: A ball thrown at the front of a stationary truck, bounces off and returns at about the same speed as it was thrown. The same ball thrown at the front of an oncoming truck bounces and returns at a greater speed than it was thrown — like a baseball bat striking a ball. A ball thrown at the rear of a departing truck returns at a reduced speed.

So it is with the radar beam. The frequency of the radio beam changes, the machine detects these changes, and, using internal circuits, translates the information into a digital readout of the speed of an oncoming or departing car.

From a driver's point of view the most disconcerting feature is that the radar speedmeter gives such limited information. When a reading comes up on the display screen it simply means that *something* is moving at the indicated rate of speed. It doesn't identify the moving object nor does it provide a precise location for that object. Thus, a police officer has to identify the object, and in making this subjective decision, the possibility of making an error greatly increases.

In order to cut down on the number of errors, police officers are instructed to visually monitor cars entering the beam. They must first believe that a specific car is travelling at an excessive rate of speed and the digital readout should only be used to corroborate that initial impression.

This is the evidence which will be acceptable to the court. In practice, however, this is not always the method. A police officer may be completing a previous ticket when suddenly the set activates and he may point to the first vehicle he sees. This is highly improper, but it will be up to you, the alleged offender, to gain as much information at the scene as possible to use in your defence.

Ask to see the readout. If the officer will not show it to

you, insist. He is not required to comply but his refusal may assist you at trial.

Take note of the area in which the officer's radar is located. Look for rotating signs, broad blade fans of the type used in large air conditioning units, large fluorescent or neon tube lights or overhead high voltage transmission lines. These can cause false readings on the display, as can nearby highway intersections or railway lines. Radio transmissions in close proximity to the radar antenna are another source of man-made interference. A taxicab or a car with a citizen's band radio could have triggered a reading on the radar set just as you came into the radar beam.

When an officer points at you, immediately take mental note of the traffic and conditions around you. It is important to be aware that radar picks up the largest object first. You may be driving at precisely the speed limit in front of a tractor trailer which is speeding. If an officer is inattentive he may incorrectly identify you as the speeding object which the radar picked up. Also note any natural sources of interference, such as heavy rain or snow. Flocks of birds or moving tree branches may also cause false readings.

For a radar determined speeding offence a police officer's evidence should include:

- his qualifications as a radar operator
- the time, date, and place where radar was set up
- his position, the road and weather conditions
- precisely when and how he calibrated the radar set
- his initial sighting of the car and his observation that "it appeared to be speeding"
- the speed registered on the radar set.

When you cross examine the police officer, here are some sample questions you might use:

- What is the make and model of the radar set?
- How was it powered?

- How does it respond to fluctuations in the power source?
- What instruments were used to calibrate the set? (*Usually tuning forks are used.*)
- When were these tuning forks checked for damage and accuracy? Who checked them? Is he present?
- When was the set last checked by a manufacturer or authorized technician?
- What types of interference, if any, can influence the set?

Remember that at trial you are only required to raise a "reasonable doubt" in the mind of the justice of the peace or judge. Therefore, if you can establish the possibility of interference or the possibility that the set was not properly maintained, he must rule in your favour.

Other Devices

Two recent innovations in the field of speed detection are also worthy of note.

The first is Mobile Digital Radar (MDR), also known as Multi-directional Radar. This device is mounted inside the police vehicle and is capable of recording the speed of another moving object while the police car itself is moving. Depending on the setting, it is possible to monitor the speed of cars going in the opposite direction or in the same direction and ahead or behind the police car. The use of this radar requires specialized training and at trial you should take pains to ensure that the officer who operated the device is properly qualified.

Another machine which is used in some states and in parts of Europe is a device called VASCAR (Vehicle Average Speed Calculator and Recorder). It is used primarily on major interstate highways. It is not a radar set, but works on the time measured distance principle to calculate a car's average speed. The police car is stopped at the side of the highway and an officer observes a car travelling at a high rate of speed. As the car passes an identifiable point on the roadway, a manhole cover or a sign, the police officer switches on a timer in the VASCAR machine. The officer also takes note of the licence number or another distinguishing feature on the car so that he can make a positive identification of it later. The police car moves out after the suspected car. As the police car passes the spot at which the timer was switched on, the officer activates another part of the machine. This part measures distance. The police officer can travel at any speed, since his vehicle itself is only measuring the distance until he catches up to the suspected car. As the car passes over another spot on the roadway, a painted line or even a long shadow, the officer switches off the timer. He switches off the distance recorder as the police vehicle passes the same spot. Instantly, the suspected car's average speed is displayed on the set calculated by the machine using the formula speed equals distance divided by time.

Many say that this device is a fairer and more accurate way of measuring a car's speed, since it is not influenced by outside interference as is radar. It gives an average speed, eliminating the "speed trap" set up at the bottom of hills, behind bushes and billboards. It is also believed to have considerable deterrent value.

With radar enforcement a driver knows he is in the clear as soon as he gets safely past a stationary radar. With VASCAR enforcement, a driver can't know if he will be pursued and stopped several kilometres after passing a police car.

An enterprising police officer in Southern Ontario invented another use for radar. Someone noticed that this officer never took a radar set out during the day but was always first in line to collect a set at night. This was a puzzle until the solution was discovered. In the early hours of the morning the inventive officer would back his car up to a building in a plaza. He would then adjust the speed monitor control on the set to its lowest setting and settle down for a snooze. If anything moved, be it a cat or sergeant, within a three hundred yard arc of the police car, the beam would pick it up and activate the alarm, warning the dormant officer. Leave it to a policeman to devise the world's most expensive wake-up system!

4
Preparing for Your Day in Court

Like all institutions, the court has a fixed procedure for getting things done. If this procedure is followed, there will be few problems. If they are not, difficulties may arise that could distract you from your purpose and frustrate your chance for a successful defence. We will answer some basic questions and show you how to get your case before the court with a minimum of aggravation.

Representation

Under the provincial acts you are entitled to be represented by an agent or a lawyer before the court. Carefully consider the situation and make your decision at the outset if you wish to seek counsel.

Find out what the penalties are for the alleged offence. Check with the ministry of transportation or equivalent in your province for applicable demerit points and the effects of a conviction on your driver's licence. Check with your insurance agent and find out what impact a conviction would have on your premiums. Bear in mind that premium increases after a conviction will generally be in place for three years. Visit a traffic court and observe what takes place.

Ask yourself if you are confident and competent enough to conduct your own defence. Many people have an inherent fear of public speaking. If you are one of these people, you might be well-advised not to take on your own defence. The courtroom setting can be intimidating and the procedures may be unfamiliar. Or you may be too emotionally involved in the facts of the case and your desire to prove your innocence.

If any of these points apply to your case, then you should seek assistance. This book can be a tool to assist you, but it cannot possibly answer all the questions you may have about your case. A qualified agent or lawyer can.

Which Lawyer or Agent

If you do not have a lawyer, you may contact your provincial law society and request that they refer one to you. Some provincial law societies have instituted a program known as 'dial-a-law' where a tape recorded message gives advice on a particular problem. If this service is available in your area it will be listed under "lawyers" in the yellow pages.

You may find some lawyers reluctant to take your case. This is understandable. A lawyer has expensive overheads and must charge for his time accordingly. To take your case and be required to appear at whatever time the court may select may be too inconvenient for him and too expensive for you. Of course, each case has its own circumstances, and each lawyer will operate differently. Some will require a substantial retainer at the outset. Others have different systems of billing. If you retain a lawyer, be sure you understand the costs involved right from the beginning. Consider experience as well as cost when choosing a lawyer. Many lawyers spend little time in traffic court and as a result their knowledge of the field may be limited.

If you prefer that someone besides yourself present your case in court, but you don't feel you need a lawyer, then an agent can represent you. An agent need not be a lawyer or even a law student, but don't ask your next-door neighbour to take on the role. An agent should be someone familiar with the type of offence and courtroom procedure. This person could be someone you know or you might ask your lawyer to suggest someone.

Another alternative in the agent's field is a new company called Pointts Limited. It is completely staffed by former police officers, who after years of enforcing the traffic laws and prosecuting cases in court, are now using their experience to help people through the traffic law maze. Professional radar operators and accident investigators will accompany you to court. Pointts Limited is located in Toronto. The telephone number is: (416) 636-5733.

Setting Dates

A pre-set date and time for your trial is normally shown on your ticket, and to plead not guilty it is necessary for you to appear and be prepared to present your defense at that time. Occasionally, however, you may be required to appear in court to "set a date" for trial, either in person or through your agent or lawyer. Your representative must be consulted before a date is set. If you have any doubts about when you are expected to appear, contact the court office.

If you intend to call witnesses, it is essential that you find out when they are available, before you make final arrangements. If you are required to set a date for trial, arrive before court is in session so that you can suggest a date to the prosecutor. He will already know what dates are convenient for his witnesses.

In some cases, the clerk may announce that only certain dates are available in that court. If that happens, and none of the dates given are possible for you and your witnesses, tell this to the judge or justice of the peace and ask for your case to be adjourned to another time to "set a date." This is an inconvenience, as it means you must appear yet again before the trial date is even set, but it is better than having to proceed when you are not prepared, or can only present a part of your case.

Adjournments

The setting of a date, or the presence on your ticket of a trial date creates an obligation to appear on that date and be ready to proceed. If something happens which makes that date unsuitable, you should inform the prosecutor immediately that you will be asking for an adjournment or (postponement) to another date.

You should fill out the request for adjournment form pursuant to the provincial acts. These can be obtained from the general office of the court where your trial is to be held. The staff will help you with the information necessary to complete this form. If you are unable to get such a form, send a letter to the prosecutor explaining your problem, so that he can decide if he has reason to oppose the adjournment or to give him a chance to cancel the appearance of his witnesses.

This procedure is preferable, because it gives the prosecutor plenty of time to adjust his plans, but it must be commenced well in advance of the date set for trial.

If an adjournment is necessary at the last moment, try to reach the prosecutor by phone, or at least leave a message with his office. You may know the name of the prosecutor from your first appearance in court, but if you don't, ask for the prosecutor in the particular court by giving the number of the court. This number will be on your ticket. But with good advance planning you can probably avoid this type of last-minute panic.

Whatever form of prior notification you use, arrive early on the originally arranged date and remind the prosecutor of your intention before court starts. Don't be caught in the position of surprising everyone with your adjournment re-

37

quest by asking for it for the first time when your case is called. Remember, it is the judge who grants the adjournment, and it is not automatic. An adequate reason is required and you should be prepared to give one. If you surprise the court, *you* may be surprised by being ordered to proceed.

Peremptory

In most cases, if your reason is valid and you have been courteous and considerate, the judge will probably allow the adjournment. However, your case will likely then be marked as "peremptory." This means that you *must* proceed on the new date without any further excuse.

Prosecution Adjournments

There is a possibility that when you arrive for your trial, you will be told by the prosecutor that the crown wishes an adjournment. (What is sauce for the goose is sauce for the gander.) If you are taken by surprise and have brought witnesses with you, oppose such a request on the grounds of inconvenience.

The prosecution may have a good reason for requesting an adjournment, such as a witness being required elsewhere, and the adjournment may be allowed. If this is the case, ask that the next date be marked "peremptory" to the prosecution. By doing so you do not prejudice your own right to a future adjournment, but if the prosecution requests an adjournment on the next date, it will not be granted. The prosecution will be forced to proceed. If the prosecution lacks evidence on account of this, the case might be dismissed.

Pre-Trial Agreed Conclusion

This term is applied to a legitimate process used by the judicial system to expedite the flow of cases through the courts.

You will sometimes hear it inaccurately referred to as "plea bargaining." What it is, is a mutually acceptable compromise between the defendant and the prosecutor, when taking a hard line on the case is not in anyone's interest. How it is used can best be illustrated by giving the following example: You are driving on a highway when you collide with the rear of another car stopped in front of you. There are no injuries and damage is slight. The police are called, however, and an investigation into the case is begun.

Assuming there are no mitigating circumstances, such as an icy road or an obstruction to your line of sight, the officer will concentrate on how long the vehicle ahead of you had been stopped. He will try to establish whether you had been driving carelessly (not paying attention to where you were going) or following too closely (not allowing sufficient distance between you and the vehicle ahead of you). This is usually determined by the evidence of the other driver, who will estimate how long he had been stopped. If it was for only two or three seconds, the inference would be that you were following too closely. If it was for a longer period of time, however, the inference is that you were not looking where you were going and were driving carelessly.

The difference between being convicted of careless driving or being convicted of following too closely is considerable, especially when such things as demerit points and insurance premiums are considered.

An officer will make his decision on the evidence he is able to gather at the scene, but should he lay a charge of careless driving against you, you would be in a very precarious situation.

If you disagree that you were driving carelessly but acknowledge that you were responsible for the collision, a possible avenue to consider is approaching the prosecutor on the date set for trial, prior to trial time, and offer to plead guilty to the lesser charge of following too closely.

The facts will be reviewed by the prosecutor and if they

are not inconsistent with evidence that could result in a charge of following too closely he may accept your plea. The matter could be concluded with a minimum of time and effort by the court.

It should be noted that these agreements are subject to the scrutiny and consent of the presiding judge. It should also be stressed that the intervention of a third party—your agent or lawyer—will considerably enhance your chances, since their credibility and reliability are already known to the court and prosecutor. They can satisfy the court and the prosecutor that an agreed conclusion will be honoured and there is no danger of a defendant using it as a device to defeat the ends of justice.

Remember, once you have entered this guilty plea, you still have the opportunity to follow the procedures outlined on page 8, dealing with entering this plea, or the plea of guilty with an explanation.

Interpreters

In recognition of the varied cultural and ethnic make-up of this country, each court has access to a pool of interpreters who speak all the major languages. These qualified interpreters are provided, free of charge, to any defendant who requests the service.

From a practical point of view, however, a defendant who requires an interpreter should seriously consider retaining an agent or lawyer to conduct his defence. Using an interpreter is like watching a movie in which the visual and sound portions are not synchronized. The defendant hears the evidence of a witness only after a delay in which the evidence is translated. The information he hears won't correspond to facial expressions or gestures that may accompany the testimony of the witness. This may make it difficult for him to concentrate on the job at hand—the gathering of information from each witness to support his argument for an acquittal.

Remember that your trial will be a one-time chance to establish your innocence. Every effort should be made to ensure that you are ready to do it right the first time.

Court Costs

There is a provision, in the provincial acts, for the awarding of court costs. There is a tendency to think of court costs in the range of thousands of dollars, because generally they are applied in civil courts with respect to law suits. But when you read the instruction sheet given to you with your traffic ticket, you will find them mentioned. You should be aware that the provision relating to court costs is very rarely invoked. It's intention is to prevent private citizens from laying false charges against each other and abusing the judicial process. In such a case, the provision for court costs acts as a deterrent in that costs may be awarded against the person laying the false charge. They may also be imposed when a person who has been convicted of an offence lodges an appeal, and the appeal obviously has no merit.

If you act reasonably and rationally in proceeding with your case, you needn't worry about being penalized by costs. In most cases these costs cannot exceed one hundred dollars even if they are levied.

The Court

The most important step now that the court is about to hear your case, is to be prepared for entering the court itself, and to understand how the court functions so you will not become confused.

The court itself is known as the Provincial Offences Traffic Court or Summary Convictions Court, depending on the province. It is not a criminal court. It does not have the power to sentence you to jail, except for contempt, non-appearance, or where expressly provided for by law. If you are facing such a charge you should be aware of it before you go to court. The address of the court will be clearly stated on your ticket, as well as the time at which court starts. You might want to make a preview visit to the court, so that you can familiarize yourself with it before your case is heard.

The first thing to remember is don't be late. If you are not there the court will start without you. You may arrive with your carefully prepared defence to find that your case has been called, you have been convicted and fined, and the prosecution witnesses have left. All you can do then is appeal, and that can be an expensive and time consuming process, with little chance of success.

On pages 53 and 54 are sketches of typical courts used for provincial offences. As you can see, there is no jury. The three people most important to you are as follows, in the order in which you will probably come into contact with them.

The Clerk

The clerk sits directly below the judge or justice of the peace. He is in charge of the paper work for all the cases to be heard in court that day. The clerk will usually be in the court fifteen minutes prior to the time court begins. The clerk will want to know you are there, so that your case can be called with as little delay as possible. But he will only know if you tell him, so you must take the initiative. Outside of the door to the courtroom the cases to be heard that day will be posted, and your case will be assigned a number on that list. Before court gets underway, check that number, then walk right up to the clerk and introduce yourself. Tell the clerk, for example, that you are Mr. John Smith and that you are here to defend your case, which is number seventeen. If there is some problem — perhaps your witnesses can't be there until 10:30 A.M., for instance — tell the clerk. Don't be intimidated by the crowds of police officers or the general crush around the clerk at the front of the court. Get to the clerk before court is in session and make your point.

The Prosecutor

The prosecutor will also be in the court about fifteen minutes prior to court-time. The prosecutor will not be gowned. He will have summaries of the cases that the crown is presenting, and lists of witnesses for each case.

It is the prosecutor, not the clerk or the judge who controls the order in which cases are called. You can't count on your case being called first, however, just because you are number one on the list. The prosecutor will be aware of scheduling problems the crown may have, and may choose to call other cases first. In most cases, the order in which the cases are called does not matter to the judge and he will not interfere.

Again, it is in your interest to introduce yourself to the prosecutor. Simply say, "I am John Smith, number seventeen on the list, and I am ready for trial." This informs the prosecutor that you are there and ready, which is helpful to him in selecting the order in which to call the cases.

This is also the time to let the prosecutor know of any problems you may have with witnesses attending. He knows that attending court is an inconvenience for people, and if he knows that your witnesses cannot be there until 10:30 A.M., your case can be moved to a time when your witnesses can appear.

If your case is called earlier than you want, it is also a good strategy to have already told the prosecutor of your scheduling difficulty. If you have told both the clerk and the prosecutor that you cannot proceed before 10:30 A.M., and your case is called at 10:20 A.M. you can tell the judge that you had requested earlier that your case be delayed until 10:30 when you expect your witnesses to appear. Then, if there are other cases waiting to proceed, the judge will probably insist on hearing them first. If you have not told anyone, the judge may be irritated with your lack of consideration and force you to proceed.

The prosecutor could be a lawyer working for the crown or he might be a police officer assigned to the courts. In any case, his function is to call your case, ensure that the evidence against you is brought before the court, cross-examine any witnesses you may call, and argue the case for conviction to the judge. We will deal with his actual presentation of the case in Chapter 5.

The Judge or Justice of the Peace

If your case is to start at 10:00 A.M., you can rest assured that the judge will not be there before that hour.

Although we refer throughout the text to the "judge," it could be either a judge or justice of the peace who actually hears your case. If it is a justice of the peace (J.P.) he or she is addressed as "Your Worship." If the judge is a Provincial Court Judge of the Criminal Division, he or she is referred to as "Your Honour." The clerk or the prosecutor can tell you which is the proper form of address on any given day. If you are not sure, or forget, address him or her as "Your Honour" and you won't go wrong.

The judge, who may or may not be gowned, is the person you must convince of the merit of your case. He or she should be treated with respect. Judges hear countless defences, good, bad, and indifferent. If you are well prepared and present your case clearly and concisely, the judge is likely to be impressed.

The Court Reporter

The court reporter makes a record of everything that is said in court. He does this either by taking shorthand or by taping it on a recorder. This is to ensure that a complete transcript of your trial is available. This is important in the case of an appeal. The judge deciding the appeal can then have before him a complete record of all that happened in your trial.

In some modern courtrooms, there is no court reporter. The clerk operates tape recorders which automatically record the proceedings of the trial. Regardless of the method used, it is important that you speak clearly.

Court Attendants

There may be a police officer or a court security officer at the back of the court. These people take no direct role in the business of the court, but are there to call cases in the halls outside the court if the call is not answered inside. They also ensure that order is maintained within the court.

Dress

Going to court is an important event. The judge should realize that you consider it important. Dress accordingly.

If you're male, dress in conservative business suit, navy blue or gray. If you don't have one, be sure to at least include a jacket and tie in your outfit. This will assure that the focus of attention is on your case, and not on you. Women are expected to be conservatively dressed was well, a suit or conservative dress will make a good impression. It is best that your clothing reflect the dignity of the court. Cut-off jeans and a sweat shirt will make an impression, but not one which is liable to help your case. Don't threaten the success of your defence over something as simple as dress.

Preparing Your Case for Court

In getting ready for your defence at trial anywhere in Canada, two things must be prepared: documents and witnesses.

Documents

Bring *all* relevant documents with you to court. The court will want to see originals, and may wish to retain copies of certain documents for its records. If you think there is any possibility they will request a copy, bring a photocopy of the document, along with the original, to court, so that you can keep the original. Your driver's licence, the ownership of the car, and your insurance certificate are all important to the court. Other documents will depend upon the nature of your case. You will be best prepared if you know in advance if the prosecutor intends to object to any of your documents, so try to check them with him at least ten days in advance. For example, if you have decided to produce documents showing how many people have been charged with the charge you are facing in the last ten years, the prosecutor may object and his objection may be upheld. You may, knowing this, decide not to produce that evidence. On the other hand, you may disagree with the prosecutor as to the relevance of the document, and, knowing he will object, you can prepare a rebuttal. What you produce must be relevant and directly to the point, but it is, finally, up to the judge to decide on the admissibility of your evidence.

Witnesses and Subpoenas

You can be certain that any police officer who is called to give evidence will be an expert witness. He has been trained to present evidence in court, and probably has done so many times. The prosecutor will also have a written summary prepared by the officer, outlining the case. You will have to be prepared for this.

You must know, too, what your own witnesses are going to say in the witness box. Review beforehand with each witness their exact recollection of the circumstances of the case. If your witness is uncertain about the sequence of events, it is better to know before you enter the court than find out during testimony, when their confusion can damage your case. If they are uncertain it may be in your best interests not to call them.

The purpose of reviewing your witnesses' evidence is to ensure an orderly presentation of your case. Your purpose is not to tell your witness what happened, but to find out what they remember. It is only fair to tell your witnesses that they may be cross-examined on what they have said. Therefore, make sure they are certain, and that they understand that you will be asking them to repeat what they remember.

Though you should review the testimony of your witnesses with them before trial, you should not attempt to "coach" them. You must realize, and know that the court realizes, that each person will have a different perspective on the same event; a different range of vision and a different emotional response. It is unwise, as well as unethical, to attempt to get your witness to substantiate your story in every detail.

Often, pedestrians or other drivers are witnesses to the event in question. Try to get their names and addresses at the scene, as well as a brief outline of what they saw. If you feel these witnesses may help your case, you should not rely on their verbal assurances that they will come to court to testify on your behalf. Their enthusiasm to aid the cause of justice may dwindle with time. For most people, appearing in court is an inconvenience, and often costly as well. They may try to avoid it despite their good intentions.

You don't want to find yourself in the situation of telling

the judge in court that your witnesses are not there, but that they said they would be. This problem can be overcome by a document known as a subpoena. A subpoena is issued by the court and it is, in fact, a summons to a witness. It works in the same fashion as a summons to a defendant; it orders the witness to appear and present whatever evidence he may have to the court. This document cannot be ignored, as it can be enforced by law. If a witness who has been served with a subpoena does not appear to give evidence, your case may be adjourned more easily than if the witness were not under subpoena. A motion for an adjournment in this case would probably be allowed, to enable you to have your witness appear at a later time. It is your responsibility to locate and notify your witness of the new date. Another subpoena need not be issued, since the original remains valid until the case is concluded.

To have a subpoena served, consult with the staff of the court office where the trial is scheduled to be held. Tell them the name and address of the person you wish to subpoena, and that you require this person to appear in court as your witness. They will then explain the procedure to follow. You should subpoena only those witnesses that you feel are essential to your case.

Motions for Dismissal

The term motion is used to describe a formal method of making a request that something in the proceedings be changed or excluded, or that the proceeding itself be terminated.

There may be a mistake on your ticket and the prosecution may put forward a "motion to amend" and you may propose on the same issue a "motion to quash." It sounds very technical, but in actual fact, motions can be very useful. It is important to know, however, that once a motion has been ruled upon by the judge, you can't repeat that motion. So every possible reason "to quash" amendments proposed by the prosecution should be investigated thoroughly beforehand. Here is an example of how you might use a motion to your advantage.

When your name is called for your case to be heard, you are expected to come forward and stand before the court, usually to the left facing the clerk and judge. The clerk will stand, ask you if you are John Smith, and read the charge. For example, the clerk may say: "John Smith, you are charged with the offence of disobeying a stop sign by failing to stop; contrary to the Highway Traffic Act, Section 116 (a). How do you plead to the charge, guilty or not guilty?"

It is at this point, *before* you have said either guilty or not guilty, that is your chance to point out to the court if there is something wrong with the charge.

In the example given, there is a serious error. The charge gives no indication of where the offence was committed. Was it in Toronto, Thunder Bay, or Medicine Hat? If you plead to this charge you will be acknowledging that it, as stated, is complete and has been properly presented to the court. Before you do so you must advise the court that you think the charge is defective because of its lack of clarity. The prosecutor will probably then suggest that the words "on James Street at Bloor Street in the Municipality of Metropolitan Toronto," or something similar, be added.

Oppose this, or any other amendments to the charge at this stage. Force the judge to make a decision. Under the provincial acts he has the power to make whatever changes are necessary in the form of the offence. But if you feel that a major element of the offence is missing, the judge may agree and dismiss the charge.

Even if the charge is correct and full as it is stated by the clerk, there are many other reasons why a charge should be dismissed, and why such a motion at this point would be successful. Charges can be dismissed if you have not been properly served. Check with your agent or lawyer. Tell them the process that was followed when you were served and they will be able to tell you if it was proper. For instance, you may be in a position to argue that you have not been properly served if the wrong copy of the ticket was given to you. If you have left the scene, and only then has the officer realized what has happened and followed you to give you the proper ticket — the judge may agree that you have been improperly served and dismiss the charge.

You also have grounds for dismissal if the wrong section number was put on the ticket. If you are charged with one offence and go to the statute books only to find that another offence is referenced by that number, the court ought to dismiss the charge. You cannot be expected to read between the lines and figure out what the officer meant to charge you with. If reading the ticket causes confusion you will not have to go through the trial.

Don't be in a hurry, however, to jump up and point out to the judge the error or confusion unless the prosecution proposes the amendment of the ticket. If the prosecution proceeds with its case and presents all of its evidence which might show, for example, that you ran through a stop sign, when the section number indicated on the ticket applies to an illegal turn infraction, the case would have to be dismissed. When the prosecution concludes its case, point out this error to the judge. It is too late for the prosecution to propose an amendment at this point, and the case would have to be dismissed. Remember that you have only one chance to make this motion and once it has been ruled upon, the issue is closed as far as the court is concerned. All your arguments for dismissal must be made at once.

It would be optimistic in the extreme to expect that because your name is "Thomson" and the ticket reads "Thompson," your charge would be dismissed. The court would consider this a minor error, and would make the amendment on the spot. If that is your sole point, and you are not calling any evidence except to make that point, your case is weak.

Each case, however, is different. What may be sufficient grounds for the court to intervene and dismiss the charge will vary from case to case. Your best guide to what the court might consider sufficient cause is an agent or lawyer. There are no hard and fast rules as to what amendments the court will allow and what it will not. Use your best judgment. Never assume the court will agree, and be prepared to proceed if the court denies your motion.

You may be sitting in the court waiting for your case to be called when you hear someone who has read this book make a motion which sounds familiar. Perhaps you had thought of trying it but had decided you were too nervous to attempt it. If you see it is successful, be flexible enough, even sitting in court waiting for your case, to change your plan and try a motion. The most successful approach is to be fully prepared, however, creative flexibility can sometimes be quite successful.

5
The Trial

Your case has been called. The charge has been read. You have pleaded not guilty, or you have made a motion for dismissal. That motion has been denied, and you have entered your plea of not guilty. The trial is about to begin. What happens now?

The Prosecution's Case

It is up to the prosecution to prove your guilt. After you have made your plea, take a seat at the defence table (see court diagrams on pages 53 and 54) and be prepared to listen to the evidence that will be called against you.

It is essential that you are prepared to hear this evidence. Bring a pad of paper and a few pens, and write down what is presented as evidence. You may find it helpful to divide a page in two: on one half write down what is said, and on the other, make notes of points you wish to challenge or mark points to be covered by your own evidence. For an example of how this is done, see page 56.

The prosecutor will call his first witness. As this witness is coming forward, you should consider making a motion to have the other witnesses excluded from the room. This may be done to prevent the prosecution witnesses from being influenced by the evidence of other prosecution witnesses.

Provincial Offences Court

(Traffic Tribunal)

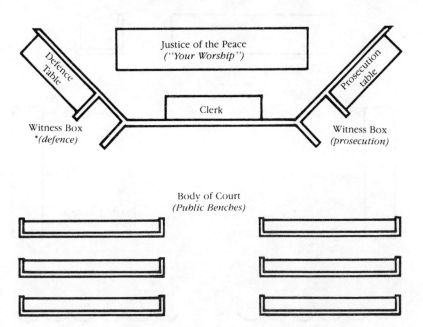

Note: There may or may not be a provincial prosecutor present in the courtroom.

* All witnesses called by the defence would give their evidence from the prosecutor witness box. Only the defendant testifies from the defence witness box.

If the prosecution has only one witness, however, and you have more than one, this motion would be to your disadvantage.

An order to exclude witnesses, granted to either side, applies to *all* witnesses, and you will be denying your witnesses

Provincial Offences Court
(Smaller towns and rural locations)

| Justice of the Peace
("Your Worship") | | Witness box |

Clerk of court

Defendant
and defence counsel's
table

Prosecutor

Prosecution table
(police officer)

Body of court
(Public seating)

the opportunity to hear all the evidence in the case. If you don't make sure that your witnesses comply, their testimony will be excluded.

If you make such a motion, and it is granted, the prosecutor may ask that the officer who gave the ticket be exempt from the order. If this occurs, request that the officer testify first, so that he doesn't have the opportunity to hear the testimony of the other witnesses. This request may or may not be granted.

The first witness, in any case, usually is the officer who

gave you the ticket. He will enter the witness box. The clerk will stand, ask the officer to take the Bible in his right hand and repeat the oath, which asks if the testimony given will be the "truth, the whole truth and nothing but the truth so help you God." The officer will say "I do" and then his evidence is ready to be heard.

If you are not of the Christian faith, you should know that the Bible used is the Christian Bible of Old and New Testaments. You can, however, be sworn in on the Jewish Bible, the Koran, or any other sacred book just as easily — if you make it available. Don't depend on the court to have a copy. Otherwise, you can be affirmed, which does not require the use of a Bible or mention the word God. It is your choice.

Now that the police officer has taken the oath, the prosecutor will ask him to explain the circumstances of the case. He will reply, for example: "I was on radar duty at 8:00 p.m. on Monday, August 20, 1984 when a car entered the beam eastbound at 80 kilometers per hour in a 50 kilometer per hour zone, on Bloor Street West, at the Humber Drive bridge, in the City of Toronto. I locked in the car, got out of my vehicle and pulled the car over. The driver stopped and identification was produced in the name of John Smith of 1234 Poplar Street, Mississauga, the accused before the court. I advised him of the offence and issued him a ticket."

You should make careful note of this evidence. If you are going to effectively cross-examine on what was said, you must *know* what was said. If you misstate the evidence, you will face the wrath of the prosecutor, the witness, and probably the judge. Remember, the judge has other cases to get to besides yours and may be impatient. He is taking notes too; make sure yours are as accurate.

The officer's evidence may be brief and general, or it may be lengthy and detailed, depending on the circumstances of the case. There are several points the officer must address in every case. The officer must establish the facts that support the charge. If the charge is 'consuming liquor in other

Charge: Failing to stop at a stop sign

	Officer's evidence
	— on duty 7 a.m. — 3 p.m. shift
	— routine traffic patrol duties
	— in scout car (marked)
	— at school crossing at stop sign (intersection)
— not fully observant of traffic	— assisting children crossing St.
	— 12:05 P.M., lunch hour group crossing
— I saw fight while stopped	— fight in schoolyard
— officer distracted by fight	— went to break it up
— no evidence saw car at intersection	— on way, observed car not stopping at sign
— 1st time noticed P.C.	— signalled to driver pull over and wait
	— broke up fight
	— returned to driver
	— id. self to driver, checked licence

John Smith
123 Main St.
Saskatoon, Sask.
Valid Sask. licence
Charged

Establish: distraction

— officer doing other things
— not directing attention to traffic
— did not observe parents following who saw me stop

56

than a residence or on licensed premises,' the officer must give evidence that proves that liquor was being consumed. The officer can't just say that he saw a bottle of beer. He must be able to testify that he saw someone drinking from it. Furthermore, the prosecution must prove that the bottle contained beer. A certificate to the effect that a chemical analysis showed the contents of the bottle to be beer must be produced for the court. (The officer cannot act as an expert on beer, and if such a certificate is not provided, the case may be defective.)

The officer also must identify you as the person charged. This is usually done by the "a.b.c. method" of pointing out the accused before the court. On occasion, however, the officer may forget this step and your case could be dismissed for "failure to identify." Although it is not really proper the judge has been known to intervene and ask, "Do you see the accused before the court?" At this point the officer will realize he has made an omission and will identify you as the person charged. Then a conviction will be in order if all else has been properly done. If you are not identified by name and as the accused before the court, the charge should be dismissed. It is essential for the prosecution to establish identity.

The evidence of the officer must also be accurate. If you have made notes at the scene as suggested in Chapter 2, and his evidence does not agree with yours, you should be prepared to cite your evidence in cross-examination.

If you see the officer referring to his notes without first asking permission from the court, you should object to his using them without first making the qualifications as to when they were made and if they have been altered since the incident. Request to read them, and if the court permits, walk over to the witness stand and read what he has written. What you might see is shown in the illustration on page 58.

Similarly, if you wish to refer to your notes when giving evidence, you must also ask permission of the court. The prosecution may also make a request to see them, and that

POLICE RECORD—COURT DISPOSITION

Date _____   ☐ GUILTY   ☐ WITHDRAWN
                        ☐ DISMISSED

SENTENCE

At 10.00am on 9 November 84 I WAS ON DUTY IN UNIFORM AND DRIVING A MARKED Police VEHICLE AND I TOOK UP OBSERVATIONS OF THE INTERSECTION OF WINONA DRIVE AND VAUGHAN Rd IN THE MUNICIPALITY OF YORK. I WAS THERE TO ENSURE COMPLIANCE WITH THE STOP SIGN SITUATED ON WINONA DRIVE. I CHECKED THE SIGN AND FOUND IT TO BE IN PLACE, CLEARLY VISIBLE AND APPARENTLY LAWFULLY ERECTED. AT APPROX. 10.25am THAT DAY I SAW A BLUE CHEVROLET MOTOR VEHICLE TRAVEL SOUTH ON WINONA DR. AND ENTER THE INTERSECTION WITHOUT STOPPING AT THE STOP SIGN. THE LIC # ON THIS VEHICLE WAS SEG 097. I STOPPED THE VEHICLE ON WINONA DRIVE AND THE DRIVER, THE DEFENDANT BEFORE THE COURT, IDENTIFIED HIMSELF AS STEVEN S. JONES.

I HAD BEEN LOCATED 15 metres WEST OF THE INTERSECTION WITH A CLEAR VIEW OF TRAFFIC APPROACHING THE INTERSECTION request may be granted. It is a good idea to be prepared for this.

Don't interrupt the evidence of the officer, even if you disagree with it. Don't stand up and say that a particular point is not correct, or accuse the officer of not telling the truth or leaving something out. The only time to interrupt occurs when the officer is about to read his summary of the conversation he had with you at the scene, from the notes he took at the time. At that point, rise and stop the proceedings.

Here you have a real opportunity to strengthen your case. Remember that the officer depends on these notes to refresh his memory. He has many cases, and the notes are essential to help him keep them straight. They may, however, be done in a hurry or compiled some time after the incident. If more than one officer is involved, the notes may be a collective effort. When this is the case, their notes will be similar, when, in fact, the officers' experiences of the incident could not be.

For example: Show five people a picture, separate them, and then ask each to write a description of what they have seen. Each description will be different. Similarly, the officers' notes should reflect those kinds of variances. If notes have been done together, the impression may be created that the results are "cooked." There is nothing wrong or improper in officers completing their notes together, however, you may be able to raise the question of what indepedent recollection each officer may actually have.

Your immediate problem, however, is the statement taken at the scene. You don't know what the officer's book contains, but by objecting to the statement before it becomes part of the evidence, you can find out. Ask to see the officer's notes. If they do not match your notes or your memory, object to their admission.

The prosecution will then have to stop its case to prove that the notes were taken from you voluntarily and with your full understanding that they could be used against you at trial.

If you felt threatened, intimidated, or forced into making a statement at the scene, you can argue against the inclusion of this evidence. Cross-examine the officer about the circumstances accompanying the taking of the statement and your apparent state of mind at the time. If you in fact did feel intimidated into making the statement, you will be invited to testify to this effect after you complete your cross-examination.

If four or five officers were involved in taking the statement, or were near enough so that their presence increased your feeling of intimidation, all of those officers must be called. The prosecution must prove that no threat of force or other intimidation was used to extract a statement from you.

It is up to the judge then to decide if the officer's statements will be allowed into the record. Failure to prove that the statement was taken from you voluntarily or failure of all of the officers involved to testify may result in the statement being excluded. Obviously this can weaken the case against you. Your use of the suggested preamble to your statement outlined on page 18 could prevent the necessity for this procedure.

The prosecution may have one witness or it may have many, depending on the case. Each witness will be called by the prosecutor and asked to describe to the court what part they had in the events under review. After each witness has finished, the prosecutor will sit down. The judge will then turn to you and ask if you wish to cross-examine the witness.

Cross-Examination

To cross-examine effectively, you must understand one basic rule: Never argue with a witness. A cross-examination is carried out by asking questions. You must know what you wish to challenge and prepare your questions to effectively

60

raise doubt about the prosecution's conclusions on the basis of the evidence or to establish the basis of your own case. You must highlight what is agreed — and what is at issue. The latter is a good preface to your own evidence.

Too many people are given the chance to cross-examine and waste it by arguing with the witness. For example, if the officer says that you were consuming liquor in a public park, you shouldn't jump up and say "I wasn't doing that." The result will be predictable. The prosecutor will object that you are not asking questions and the judge will become testy and agree, and will remind you to ask questions.

It is probably best to keep your cross-examination short. This will be more effective, and your points can be made directly. Don't repeat yourself. Before you go into court write down the questions that must be asked. You will then have an outline of what you need to do. You should then add to it any questions that arise out of the officer's evidence.

There is no set pattern of how to cross-examine. You will know your own case best. In the instance just described, however, a question you could ask might be, "Where were you standing when you first saw me?" This is a proper question and will bring a relevant issue into focus; the element of where the offence occurred. See if the officer will then agree with you on certain facts. For example, a question which will establish facts might be: "Would you agree with me that I was in a group of seven people and the light was poor at that time?"

It is possible to put your entire case to the officer in the form of questions. Establish areas of agreement and of dispute. This will serve two purposes. First, it will show the judge where the disagreement lies. Second, it will give him the basic thrust of your argument. Then, when you present your evidence, the judge will hear these same points. They will be put before him yet again when you summarize your case in argument. By then, the judge will be thoroughly familiar with your version of the events in question.

In some cases, it may be necessary to go into a more detailed and technical cross-examination. Radar is such an area. Radar is not infallible and police officers are given instruction manuals outlining standard questions that may be asked regarding their use of it. The answers to these questions are also provided. These are not, however, the only questions that can be asked. But the questions you might need to ask can involve you in a technical cross-examination. In this type of case, you should seriously consider retaining an agent or lawyer, especially if the consequences of a conviction could be serious.

If you're conducting your own cross-examination, stick to the point. Don't get angry and quell any impulse you may have to make slighting comments about the officer's competence. When you are finished, thank the officer and sit down. Courtesy never hurts your case.

Re-examination

After you have completed your cross-examination, the prosecutor has the right to re-examine the witness before he leaves the stand. The purpose of this re-examination is to clarify points that may have been weakened or challenged by your cross-examination. However, the prosecutor cannot at this point bring out new evidence. He can't introduce, for example, a fact he forgot to mention at first. If you think this is happening, object. If you don't object and this new evidence goes into the record you have no further right of cross-examination.

When the prosecutor has completed his re-examination, the judge may then choose to question the witness. If he does, and as a result new evidence emerges, he will invite you and the prosecutor to examine the witness on this new evidence.

For example, suppose you have been charged with speeding and the officer's evidence was that the radar device which he used indicated that you should be charged. At the end of the re-examination, the judge asks what type of device it was. This question had not been raised earlier. The officer answers naming the device. The judge then asks if there are any questions arising out of this new evidence.

You then remember that you had forgotten to ask this question and several others related to it. You should ask every question that comes to mind. In this case you may be able to question the accuracy of a machine of this type; perhaps other machines of this type have been unreliable, perhaps the equipment is considered obsolete and is no longer being purchased. You can elicit any such information under these circumstances.

The witness will now be dismissed and will leave the witness box. The next witness will be called and the process is repeated. Again, take careful notes and cross-examine as you did for the first witness. Repeat this process for all the prosecution witnesses.

You can never know what witnesses the prosecution will call. In most cases it will be only the officer who laid the charge. But if other witnesses are called, you must be prepared. On the other hand, the prosecution will not know what witnesses you may choose to call.

The Defence

After all the prosecution's witnesses have been called the judge will turn to you and ask you to present your defence. You may wish to move that the charges be dismissed, at this point, but only in rare cases will this be successful. For example, if no evidence has been produced to prove a necessary element of the charge, the case may be dismissed.

Suppose you have been charged with careless driving. The prosecution witnesses have given evidence that establishes it was your car that was involved and it was being driven in a careless manner. None of them, however, has identified you as the person who was driving. As such, the case against you has not been proved. The prosecution has not established a "prima facie" case; that is, all the necessary facets have been covered. Before you begin your defence, tell the judge why you believe the case against you is defective and ask that it be dismissed.

What must be proven in each case is different but prosecution witnesses, especially police officers, are expert witnesses. It is very rare for a major omission to be made, but it does occur. If you think that an omission has been made which goes to the heart of the matter, make your statement as briefly as possible. In the example given you might rise and say:

> "Your Honour, this case should be dismissed. There is no evidence of any kind as to the identity of the driver. No witness has indicated the driver in the court and no witness has even described the appearance of the driver. Therefore, there is no evidence before the court that the defendant was in fact the driver. The case should be dismissed."

The prosecution will then be allowed to respond to your argument. The prosecution will very likely assert that a case has been made which requires a defence to answer it. Any omission will be downplayed and your objection will be dismissed as an annoyance. The provincial acts will be cited. It will sound impressive and maybe intimidating.

The judge will then expect you to reply to the argument of the prosecutor. Don't be intimidated. Repeat that no matter what the judge has heard, an essential flaw exists in the prosecution's case, namely the omitted items, and as the prosecution has closed its case, it is the duty of the court to either allow the case to be re-opened and corrected or the case should be dismissed. Repeat that you believe the court should dismiss the case.

It is now the judge's decision and he may or may not decide in your favour. Your chances are better if the judge has a long list of cases still to be heard that day. Your defence will take time, and if the day's caseload is heavy, the judge may be just as happy to dispose of one matter quickly. This is a sad comment on the administration of justice, but it is all too true in many cases. If he decides in your favour, the case is dismissed and you are free to go. If he decides against you, you will be called upon to proceed.

In any event, your defence has already been prepared. Again, never assume that the case will be dismissed and you will not have to call a full defence.

You will probably be your own first witness, unless time constraints on your other witnesses force you into calling one of them first. You will be sworn in by the clerk and will go to stand in the witness box. You may be offered the choice of sitting while giving evidence. Don't. You will appear more in control and confident if you stand. Also, your voice projects better from a standing position.

You know the prosecution's case now, so make certain that your defence challenges the points of evidence that have been made against you. Tell your story from the beginning and set the facts in their proper context. Sometimes the presentation will put a completely different picture on a case. For example, suppose the prosecution has presented a case against you for speeding. The officer may not have mentioned that you were rushing an expectant mother to the hospital. You are able to present evidence from the hospital which proves that this was, in fact, what you were doing. In the unlikely event that you should be convicted in such a case, your presentation of this evidence would produce a very different penalty than one which might otherwise have been imposed.

Remember in giving your evidence that it is the judge that you have to impress, not the prosecutor. Speak directly to the judge. Begin your evidence with "Your Honour" or

"Your Worship." Then, as clearly and as concisely as possible, tell your story to the court. Explain events as they occurred, describing them as well as you can. Don't try to argue your case at this point; that will come later. Simply give your side of the story, succinctly, and without embroidering in any way.

When you have finished, say so. You will then have the dubious pleasure of being cross-examined on your version of events. At this point, it will be clear to the prosecutor where your version diverges from the version of the prosecution witnesses, and these will be the areas of particular concern to him. The purpose will be to test your memory of events against those of the officer and his notes on the incident. He will try to make you admit that your memory is not as reliable as the notes of the officer on the scene. He may question you on side issues or details you have mentioned, hoping to demonstrate that your memory is not reliable. For instance, he might point out that although you mentioned there were four officers at the scene, there were, in fact, only three. This is a good reason not to try to stretch your memory. If you think you remember a detail, but are not certain and it is not essential, it is best to leave it out. Chances are that it will not help, and it may hurt your case. You don't want to weaken your case over a minor point.

During the course of cross-examination, you may find that the prosecutor becomes confused. This is understandable, as the prosecutor has many cases to keep straight. You may be tempted to assist the prosecutor, to help him clarify the issues. Don't. The judge won't give you extra credit for being helpful beyond the call of duty and the confusion of the prosecution may actually work in your favour. The wrath of the bench for a confused cross-examination will fall on the prosecution, not on you, and from your perspective that is an unexpected bonus.

At the conclusion of the prosecution's cross-examination the judge may have additional question for you. Don't be evasive or defensive either in cross-examination or in reply to a question from the bench. The best answer is short, truthful, and direct. If the judge wants detail, he will ask for it. Usually questions from the bench are asked to help the judge understand an area cloudy to him, or to clarify facts that cross-examination may have confused. Look the judge squarely in the eye when you address the bench. It is the judge you must impress with the righteousness of your case.

When he completes his questioning, you will be excused from the witness box. You will be asked if you have any other witnesses to call. Call your first witness, ideally the person who is next closest to the facts and following the outline you have made of your defence.

The witness will be sworn in, and the judge will indicate that you may proceed. Ask the witness to explain his involvement with the case; what was seen and done, where and when the events occurred, and what view he had from his physical vantage point of the circumstances that are relevant to the case. This evidence emerges only from questions that you put to the witness, so be certain that not only do you know what answers he will give, but that these answers will clearly represent your side of the case. If you intend to enter any exhibits, such as notes the witness may have taken at the scene, hold them up, ask the witness to identify them, show them to the prosecutor and then ask that they be filed as exhibits.

Again, it is important never to be surprised by the answers of your witness. Nothing is worse than an unexpected response. A trial develops a momentum of its own and if you are caught unprepared by evidence, it will show. You may become confused and nervous and this will defeat your aim of a clear, concise presentation highlighting your disagreement with the case put forward by the prosecution.

When you have finished questioning your witness, the judge will call upon the prosecutor for cross-examination of your witness. You should warn your witnesses that they will be subject to cross-examination, and as this may be an unpleasant process for them you should take some care to advise them of what to expect.

Each witness should know that in cross-examination, the purpose of the prosecutor's questions will be to cast doubt on the value of their testimony especially where it diverges from the testimony of the prosecution's witnesses. This can be done in as many ways as there are prosecutors. In some cases, the prosecutor will try to show that your witness is shading the truth in your favour. This can take the form of direct accusations that the witness is not being truthful, or it can be a more subtle process where the prosecutor will attempt, detail by detail, to demonstrate weakness, inaccuracy, or omission in the evidence given. The latter approach is longer, more methodical, and less emotional, but it can be just as exacting, if not more so. At each step, the witness's evidence is challenged and the suggestion made that his view or reaction could not be as accurate as that of the witness for the prosecution.

It will be different for your witness than it was for the officer. The officer is used to being cross-examined and may even look upon it as something of a challenge. Your witnesses, on the other hand, may become a little exasperated or testy when their motives or observations are called into question. It is important to prepare them for this. They should be aware that cross-examination is no picnic, and can be a rather trying ordeal. Assure them that the best thing to do is relax as much as possible and not attempt to fight the prosecutor or guess where his questions are leading. Tell them to simply try to answer the questions in the most straightforward and open way possible.

When cross-examination is completed, you are entitled to ask your witnesses questions in re-examination. Re-examination evidence is one of the most misunderstood areas of the trial. Remember, though, that the same rules apply to you as applied to the prosecution in the case of re-examination. You are not allowed to present information that you may have forgotten in your original questioning, or ask questions unrelated to areas covered in cross-examination. What you want to do is confront issues that may have been blurred by cross-examination. Reinforce your case with questions meant to clarify the confused areas.

Suppose you have been charged with running through a stop sign. The evidence of your witness, a passenger in your car, was that you stopped, but in cross-examination the prosecutor tried to show that the attention of the witness was distracted by a jet passing overhead, and therefore he could not say for certain if the car had stopped or not.

Because you were present, you know the answers you will get if you ask the right questions. In re-examination you might ask the following:

Q. "You have heard the prosecutor suggest that you were distracted by a jet passing overhead and cannot say that I stopped at the sign. I would like to ask you where the car was in relation to the intersection when you observed the jet?"
A. "Stopped at the stop sign."
Q. "How can you say that for certain?"
A. "Because you saw the plane first, stopped the car at the stop sign and pointed it out to me."

Obviously, the questions are not likely to be that easy. In any event, you should be aware that you can refer to the questions and answers given on cross-examination to ask for clarification.

A favourite trick of a cross-examiner is to stop a witness before the witness has the chance to fully explain the answer or put it into the proper context. If you noticed this in cross-examination, you could say in re-examination:

"In cross-examination, you were asked about X and said Y in reply. Would you tell me the context in which you gave that answer, or would you like to expand that answer?"

Repeat what was asked in cross-examination and then the answer given, and ask for clarification or expansion of that answer. Questions such as; "Do you have anything to add to that?" or "Would you care to comment on that answer?" will give your witness the opportunity to collect his thoughts and possibly resolve the ambiguity left by the prosecution's cross-examination.

In re-examination be concise. It is useful to tell the judge that this is your intention. Say, for example; "Your honour, I will be brief in re-examination." and then follow through. The court will appreciate it. Deal only with the major points made in cross-examination or you may get confused, and ask questions which aren't proper re-examination. Remember not to bring up new issues. The last thing you want at this point is the prosecutor objecting to your questions.

When all your witnesses have testified, the prosecutor has the right to call further evidence, in what is called *reply*. This is rarely used in traffic court, but is completely up to the prosecutor's discretion. In a reply witnesses may be called to address issues raised by the defence that can be replied to by prosecution evidence. You will have the opportunity to cross-examine any such witness.

The Argument

With the completion of the evidence, the time has come to present the arguments to the court. The judge will turn to you and ask you if you have any submissions.

You should have prepared an outline of the points you wish to make in argument before you go to court. Outline your case as briefly as possible, covering your main points and highlighting the key aspects of your defence. Cite your own testimony and that of your witnesses, contrasting it to the testimony of the prosecution witnesses. Point out why your testimony is preferable, whether it is because your witnesses had a better view of the events, or for any other reason that may be convincing.

The keynote here is to summarize, not to rehash all the evidence. Remember, the judge has heard it all and has made notes, and the last thing he wants is to hear it again. He is looking for guidance at this point. What insight can you give to the evidence before the court? This is the crucial question.

Keep you argument focused on the main issues. Avoid any tendency to become sidetracked on minor points. (If, however, the handling of minor points highlights a contrast between your crisp presentation and a confused case presented by the prosecution, you may want to bring this to the attention of the court. Otherwise, ignore them and deal directly and exclusively with the main issues in contention. In the end, this is where your case will stand or fall.) You may find it helpful to summarize your argument to the bench before you go into detail. You might do this in the following manner: "Your Honour, I submit that there are three reasons that this charge should be dismissed. They are the following..." Then state your arguments in order. After outlining your reasons, return to the first argument and deal with it in detail, and then do the same for the second and the third. Conclude your argument with something like this: "Therefore, Your Honour, for the three reasons I outlined to you, I submit that the charges should be dismissed." Use the word "submit," as opposed to "suggest," "feel," or "would you not agree?" "Submit" is a confident word, and states your conviction clearly and firmly. Uncertainty, at this point, should be avoided at all costs.

At any point in the course of your argument, the judge may interrupt you for clarification, or to agree with you and speed you along to your next point. If you are certain that this is his intention, move to your next point. If a question comes from the bench, halt your argument and answer it.

Sometimes such a question is one that you are expecting to answer in the next few points. If that is the case tell the judge that you are coming to that. When you reach the point he asked about, remind him of his question, and ask: "Is Your Honour's question answered?" If it isn't, you should answer it right away. If it is, the judge will say so and you can move on, secure in the knowledge that the issue is clear.

Never argue with the judge. You can't win such an argument. Treat the court with respect at all times. Answer all questions from the bench as openly and completely as possible.

When you have completed your argument, sit down. The court will then ask the prosecutor to present his argument in reply. The prosecutor will address your argument and try to persuade the court that it is deficient and should be rejected. This may or may not be a lengthy process, depending on the inclination of the prosecutor. You should not interrupt unless you hear an obvious misstatement of the evidence. If you do, get to your feet and advise the court that the statement is not correct, and state what the evidence was, that was put before the court. The value of good notes will be evident here. If you are confident enough and believe your notes to be accurate, invite the judge to compare his notes of the evidence with yours.

Normally, however, you will just listen to the prosecutor summarize the case of the prosecution and aruge for a conviction. The judge may also question the prosecutor, as he questioned you. When the prosecutor sits down, the case is formally concluded. You cannot add anything more, unless the judge requests that you do so.

Don't be upset if you notice that the court reporter (if there is a court reporter) is not recording your argument. The argument is generally not recorded, unless the judge requests it. It doesn't mean that an incomplete record will be compiled. The "record" is the transcript of the evidence, together with any exhibits that have been filed. The argument is not normally considered part of the transcript.

The Judgement

This is the climax of the whole process. The judge now weighs the evidence, and his words are final. Unless spoken to, you say nothing. Listen carefully and write down as much of the judge's speech as you can. If he decides against you this information may prove useful in considering an appeal.

The judge has heard a complete case from both sides, and usually the judgment will begin by repeating the charge and a summary of the facts as presented in evidence. He may comment on the evidence of the witnesses individually or collectively, and then will come to his conclusion, either registering a conviction or dismissing the charge.

If the charge is dismissed, you have been cleared and are free to leave. If a conviction is registered, the penalty may be a fine, imprisonment, or both, but the judge usually has at this point a discretion or choice as to what penalty is within the limits prescribed by the law. He will then ask you if you have any submissions as to penalty. By this he means that he wishes you to advise him of any reasons there might be which would mitigate the sentence he is about to pass. He wants to know at this point if you have been before the court before, or if you need your car to make a living. Take advantage of this last oppportunity to impress the judge with your sincerity and your reasonable approach to the fact that you have been found guilty.

Sentencing

If you are convicted, the judge can impose the following penalties:

Suspended Sentence. A conviction is registered, but no fine is imposed.

Suspended Sentence; Conditional on Attendance to a Driver Education Program. A conviction is registered but no fine is imposed *provided* you attend a driver education class, which consists of a movie and discussion of safer driving habits. These classes are run by the ministries of transportation for each province. If you don't attend within the required time limits, the penalty will be reassessed, and you will have to pay a fine. (Once an elderly defendant was before the court having been convicted of an accident related offence. When he was asked if he had ever had a driver education course, he replied, "The wife's been giving me one ever since the accident.")

Minimum Fine. A conviction is registered but you are given the minimum fine, usually considerably lower than the fine shown on the face of your ticket.

Set Fine Imposed. A conviction is registered and you must pay the fine shown on the face of the ticket.

If in the court's opinion the circumstances merit it, a greater fine, up to a maximum of two thousand dollars, can be imposed. It is also possible for a judge to suspend your licence for a period of up to two years. Fortunately these occasions are rare.

After conviction you will be asked if you have anything to say about your sentence or penalty. Prepare for this moment before you come to court. If the fine is a hardship, speak up and explain your circumstances. Don't be embarrassed; it happens hundreds of times a day and you will find the court sympathetic to your situation.

As stated earlier, demerit points are automatically assessed and are not under the court's jurisdiction. The court has no authority to change them.

All fines are due within fifteen days of being imposed, unless you request additional time to pay or permission to make the payment in installments.

6
Appealing the Decision

Despite your best efforts, either personally or through an agent or lawyer, and despite the great weight of your arguments, justice has turned a blind eye and you have been found guilty as charged. Sentence has been imposed, but in the pit of your stomach you have a feeling that you have been had. Justice has erred, and you want even yet to set the record straight. Therefore you decide to appeal to a higher court. You must do so within a specified time period, so check with your agent or lawyer, or look up the appropriate statute under appeals for the deadline which applies.

This decision involves you in a completely different set of circumstances, and in a different forum. How far and how long you can appeal is up to you, the limits of the law, and your own finances. Recently, a parking ticket issued in Manitoba ended up in the Supreme Court of Canada on the issue that it was not in French. It resulted in a decision that all the laws of Manitoba for the past century should be in French as well as in English. Admittedly, this was an extraordinary case and does not represent the common experience.

The time involved in preparing and conducting an appeal can vary from one area to another. In some provinces the appeal process can be completed in several weeks, although in other areas it may be months before your case reaches the courts for a hearing.

It is not always necessary to seek professional help before making a decision to appeal. In most cases, however, it is probably good advice. Even if you have conducted your own case, and have done a competent job, the appeal process is more complex and technical, and as it may be your last chance to have your conviction overturned, you would be well advised to make use of a professional. Initial consultation with an agent or lawyer need not be expensive, and they can give you their expert opinion on whether you have grounds for a successful appeal. They can also bring a fresh approach to your problem.

Once you have made the decision to appeal, it is important to understand what the subject of an appeal can be and what the judge hearing the appeal will allow. You need to understand the following in order to gauge your chances for a successful appeal.

What Can Be Appealed

You can appeal the decision on two bases, namely, that the decision was made with no proper basis in the evidence, or that the decision made was wrong about a point of law. There are other bases — that the court hearing the matter did not have the jurisdiction to do so, or was biased in some tangible way, to name two examples — but these are rare.

Appeals Regarding Facts

This is a difficult case to appeal. The judge has heard the evidence from the witnesses directly and therefore the facts should be readily available to him when he makes his decision. Judges, however, all too often prove themselves to be completely human, and, as a result, facts become distorted, exaggerated, or completely ignored when the decision is delivered. It is possible in some cases that there was a complete absence of evidence to support the decision that was made. You were found guilty of consuming liquor in a park, however, the judge failed to ask the prosecution to prove that what was shown to be a person drinking from a bottle was actually the same thing as consuming *liquor*.

Generally, the other ground on which an appeal regarding facts may be successful is to argue that although there was some factual evidence to support the finding of the judge, the finding was so completely unreasonable based on the interpretation of the facts at hand, that in the interests of justice it cannot be allowed to stand. The charge was serving liquor to a minor; however, though the defendant appeared to be under age, no evidence of age was actually given. Therefore, despite the fact that a conviction was registered, an appeal could succeed.

No Evidence to Support the Decision

This can arise in many ways. For example: An officer had stopped a car and was investigating the driver. Suddenly, another car went by at what the officer perceived to be a higher rate of speed than the law allowed. The officer followed the second car, a "chase" that did not take long. A ticket was given for doing 70 km/h in a 60 km/h zone.

At trial, the charge against the second driver was disputed. The driver was convinced that he was going 60 km/h and he could not understand how the officer could say that he was going 70 km/h when no radar was used. Besides, the driver pointed out, the officer was used to traffic passing him at the normal city speed of 50 km/h. Wasn't it natural that 60 km/h would seem faster than normal? And wasn't it true that the officer had no difficulty catching the driver very soon after leaving the scene of his initial investigation?

Despite all this evidence to the contrary, the judge made the following decision, which is not atypical; "This is an experienced officer, and I am satisfied that the case has been proven. There will be a conviction."

When you are deciding on an appeal, the importance of the notes you took during the trial becomes apparent. If you took extensive notes, you will be able to tell if there were any facts upon which the conviction could be based. If, on the other hand, you were so confident that your case would be successful that you did not bother to take complete notes, your ability to prove that the court made a decision with no evidence to support it is seriously reduced.

In the example given, the judge has not made any comment on the evidence. He has made a comment on the officer. This is not necessarily a rare circumstance. It may be your first time before court. Chances are that the officer has been in court many times. Because of this, especially in rural areas, judges get to know the police officers who come before them on a regular basis. It is only natural that a judge will come to respect the manner in which some officers give their evidence. And it is only natural that the judge will give the benefit of the doubt to the police officer. This happens often enough that it is recognized as a characteristic of the judicial system. It is not to say that the system is prejudiced, or stacked against the defendant. But the system is run by people, after all, with all their imperfections. It is perfectly natural that a relationship will build up, over time, between the bench and the police officers. At times, it means that the bench will not permit laxity on the part of the police. At times, it can operate against a defendant.

Regardless of the judge's confidence in the testimony of the police officer, however, such a decision is groundless. Whether the officer is the chief of police or a rookie, the case must be decided on its own merits. A decision which ignores all of the evidence has not addressed the requirements of proof necessary for a conviction. An appeal of this case has a good chance of success.

When to make your appeal will always be a sensitive

decision. If you have prepared your case carefully and thoroughly, made all the points you intended to make, cross-examined effectively, and argued well, and the decision has still gone against you, your natural reaction is that justice has not been done. In the emotional storm that may result, you may impulsively decide to appeal. At the appeal stage, you may find that the higher court judge tells you the matter is simply a question of credibility and your appeal is therefore dismissed.

You have just been taught a hard lesson. On a question of strict credibility, your chances of winning an appeal are slim. In other words, if at trial the judge had two versions of the facts from which to choose — you say that you were not speeding; the officer says you were—and the judge accepted the officer's evidence, on appeal it is up to you to show that the judge's choice was completely unreasonable. An appeal is like taking the decision of a lower court to a higher one and proving to the satisfaction of that court that the decision itself is unsound. You do not get another trial on appeal, and the judge will not hear your witnesses. All he can do is judge the judgment, and in the case of credibility alone, he will rely on the best judgment of the lower court.

It is not a question of credibility, however, if you brought three witnesses who swore that you were not speeding, and the judge in his decision made no reference to their evidence. The court in that case has ignored the evidence given, and you can argue on appeal that the lower court's decision was unreasonable.

Also, if you can show the appeals court that the evidence of the prosecution had an obvious lack of unity or clarity, and the evidence of the defence was clear and to the point and yet the judge chose to accept the case of the prosecution, you may have a successful appeal. For example, if two police officers were involved in the case and they gave conflicting or unsubstantiated evidence, the case of the prosecution may have been so flawed that the judge's decision in its favour was completely unreasonable. An appeal of the decision may well succeed.

Evidence Incapable of Supporting Conviction

Your conviction can be reversed on appeal if the appeal judge can be persuaded that the judge at the trial dealt with the evidence in a way that made it incapable of supporting the verdict. This is not as clear cut an area as when there is no evidence to support a conviction, so you must weigh your situation with great care before you decide to launch an appeal.

For instance, in the example given, the judge may have said, "This is an experienced officer. He has said that it looked to him like the defendant was speeding and he guessed the defendant was going 70 km/h. There will be a conviction."

As you can see, this type of case presents a different problem. The judge has made a determination, and has convicted the defendant *based upon that determination*. But what was that initial determination based upon? If the defendant has been skillful in the cross-examination of the police officer and capable in presenting his overall defence, the judge may have had no basis to that determination. The bald statement of the officer that he guessed that the defendant's car must have been speeding should not be sufficient. If that is so, and the court of appeal is shown that there is no hard evidence to support the conviction, the court may allow that the case should have been dismissed and the appeal will be successful.

Again, to determine this good notes are necessary. These notes would have been taken when the judge made his decision, and reviewing them will indicate whether or not the judge had a basis for the decision, and whether it is capable of supporting a conviction.

Costs vs. Consequences: Making the Decision

An appeal may be your last chance, and should be very carefully considered. For example, if the conviction was for careless driving and a conviction means that you will lose your licence, it is crucial to consider the appeal process. However, there are two factors which will come into play on an appeal. One is cost. The other is the chance of success. These are not as good as they are at trial.

You should not embark upon the trial process casually, with the idea that you can always appeal. The consequences of your conviction may still take place even while your appeal is underway. In Ontario, for instance, you remain convicted until an appeal court removes the conviction. After all, you have been found guilty. In some jurisdictions, however, if the judge at the trial so directs, you may be able to keep your licence until the appeal has been heard and it has been determined that the conviction will stand. For the exact status of your record, pending an appeal's hearing, consult an agent or lawyer. In most cases, however, the court will allow the consequences to stand to discourage frivolous appeals.

You should consider carefully the cost of an appeal. You must have another day in court for a start, and you must become prepared for that day. At the very least, an appeal will interrupt your everyday schedule and interfere with your life.

Most people don't enjoy finding themselves in court. The trial itself is bad enough — the appeal process is worse. At the appeal level, you are not dealing with an assortment of witnesses, you will be confronting one judge and one lawyer who will represent the prosecution. If you are preparing to undertake the appeal yourself, remember that you will be entering an even stranger environment than the first trial. And if you decide to be represented by an agent or by a lawyer, you will be shouldering the burden of considerable expense, compounded if the agent or lawyer did not represent you at the first trial, as he has to take over and argue a case which was not prepared or presented by him in the first place. You will also have to pay to get a transcript of evidence; the verbatim recording of everything that happened at your trial.

To begin the appeal process and add it to the court list, you must fulfill numerous technical requirements. First of all, you must advise the appeal court that you want to appeal the decision. This is done by filing a Notice of Appeal with the appropriate court office, which can be hard for someone who is not familiar with the court process. The appeal office of the court may be in a different part of the court building, or it may be in another building. In all cases, you will need to file a formal Notice of Appeal. To do this, go to the court office where you have been instructed to go to pay your fine upon your conviction. Ask the people there where you can obtain a Notice of Appeal and follow the instructions given. If you are not successful, phone the prosecutor's office and they should be able to give you instructions. If that doesn't work, contact the attorney-general's office and ask for assistance.

You must then contact the court to order the transcript. Make sure that it is available on the date it is needed and that it will go to the correct court. There is nothing more embarrassing than showing up in court and finding out that you have failed to meet one of the requirements necessary for the appeal to be heard. The court will already be unfavourably disposed towards you by the time the appeal can begin. And, obviously, if you have retained an agent or a lawyer you will have to pay for yet another slice of their time.

The Appeal

In an appeal you must know what to say. A line like "I wasn't guilty, the judge didn't understand" will conclude your case very quickly. What the appeal court judge wants to hear is not the argument of your case (which, after all, has already failed once), but a good reason why he should intervene now. Long rambling monologues about the shortcomings of the testimony from the witness for the prosecution is not going to endear you to the judge, nor will it win you your appeal. Do your homework and present your case as concisely and convincingly as you can.

The traffic appeal court is a different court than the regular traffic court as you can see by the diagram on page 84. Don't be alarmed by the impatience that you'll notice in the appeal court. When your case is called, rise and introduce yourself as the defendant in the case before the other court (which you should name), now appearing as the party appealing in this court. Then state your case in a form something like this: "Your Honour, there are a number of reasons that this appeal should succeed. They are as follows: First, the judge misunderstood the evidence and came to a conclusion which cannot be supported by the evidence before the court; and second, the judge erred in law in concluding that the speed of my car could be established by the mere guess of a police officer, without any supporting proof or means of verification. I would like to begin with my first point."

If the appeal is presented in this fashion, the court will draw a few conclusions. First of all, it will recognize that you know what you are doing and that you are prepared. Imagine the number of times the court is confronted by an aggrieved person who, having decided to appeal, obviously is baffled by the process in which he is involved. Very quickly the judge will grow restless, and the unwitting appellant will soon find himself back on the sidewalk wondering what happened. By impressing the court with your competence right away, you've won your first battle.

Presenting several key points, as opposed to a lengthy list

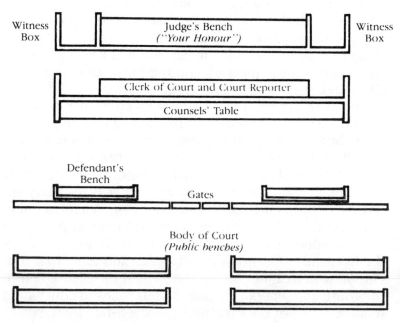

Note: This court is always presided over by a provincial court judge
who may or may not be robed.

of arguments, will also be appreciated by the court. Remember, if your best arguments will not win the case for you, your less important points are unlikely to persuade anyone either. The idea is to recognize what your best points are and dispense with those that are less effective.

Several years ago, a prominent Toronto lawyer was fully prepared to take a serious case to the Supreme Court of Canada in Ottawa. Before the date to file the appeal, he approached another eminent lawyer and asked the older man to review his summary of the points he intended to argue. The elder man was appalled to see that the lawyer intended to argue thirty-two points of law. He took him aside and asked him which were his best three points. He then advised the younger man to discard the other twenty-nine points. They might be of some interest to legal scholars or zealots, he explained, but they were unlikely to persuade the nation's highest court. The younger man took his advice.

Put yourself in the judge's position for a moment. If someone stands before you and announces that he has thirty-two points for you to hear, and those points are not even ranked, how would you feel? Probably discouraged, at least, especially when you see the wad of paper that he intends to wade through. Suppose, on the other hand, the person stands before you with a small note pad and explains that he has two points to make, which he hopes will help you evaluate the appeal? He then proceeds to crisply summarize the points and outlines their significance in the broader context of the case. If you were the judge, you would be likely to prefer this approach far more than the first. A good argument well presented is guaranteed to have more effect than a good argument badly presented — and infinitely more effect than a bad argument badly presented.

The argument on a traffic ticket offence at the appeal stage should not be lengthy. You should be able to make your best arguments in ten to fifteen minutes. It is then up to the judge to question you on any point he wants clarified. Again, as in the trial process, remember that the purpose of this exercise is to win over the judge. You are not being questioned by the bench as a form of harassment. The judge wishes to understand a point, or test your ability to project what effect a particular point would or should have on his decision.

Make sure you understand each question the judge asks before you try to answer. If a portion of the question is not clear or you do not hear it entirely, ask the judge to repeat it.

After you have answered as best and completely as you can, it is not out of order to ask the judge if he is satisifed that the question has been answered. If the judge is still not satisfied, you will then have an opportunity to resolve whatever degree of doubt which may remain in his mind. Remember to leave no stone unturned. Chances are that the case will end with his judgment. Make sure that for you it ends at the right point, with nothing unresolved.

When you finish your presentation, it will be the turn of the prosecution to respond to your points. Just as at trial, listen carefully to the prosecutor's rebuttal. The argument by the other side will be fairly standard in an appeal situation. Basically, what will be said is that the decision at the trial level was correct. The prosecution will point to the elements of the offence that had to be proved and then try to show that those elements had, in fact, been proven. Your arguments will be addressed and in most cases dismissed as insignificant or irrelevant to the true nature of the case before the court.

Do not become angry because the prosecutor belittles your best points. Listen carefully to his arguments and make careful note of each detail. Do not interrupt unless the prosecutor tries deliberately to mislead the court. If you are sure this is the case, jump up and indicate this to the court with all the force you can muster. But if you do this, be correct. There is nothing worse than arousing the anger of an otherwise sympathetic judge by interrupting without cause. On the other hand, you cannot allow evidence to be misstated. The line is a thin one, but in the final analysis it is better to err on the side of caution. If you are uncertain if the line has been crossed, do nothing. You can always try to set things right in reply, if you consider it necessary. You may decide that the arguments made are so weak that nothing can be gained by speaking again.

When their case is closed you will have the opportunity to respond to the arguments of the other side. This is not the time to restate your entire case. What the judge wants to hear is your perception of the problems in the argument presented by the prosecution. Be very brief and very much to the point. Tell the judge exactly what you object to in the prosecution's argument. Restate the argument succinctly and tell the court why it is not correct. The clearer you are, the better. The judge by now understands both sides.

The purpose of reply is to make your last comments on what has been said, not on the case in general. If you have made a point and the other side has not addressed it, you can refer to that point again and remind the court that it was not challenged. Don't review the entire argument, merely remind the court that it was not challenged and so it should stand.

It is good style to summarize your intentions to the judge first, especially if you are not an agent or lawyer. As you get up to deliver your reply, make a statement something like this: "Your Honour, I have two points to make in reply to the arguments you have just heard, which can be stated briefly." This achieves several things. First of all, it lets the judge know that you are not going to argue your case again. Secondly, it tells him that you feel that there are only a few points that have been made that require a response. Thirdly, it indicates that your reply argument will not be long and wandering, but concise and to the point.

After you have made your last point, pause and look for a reaction from the judge. In ninety-nine cases out of a hundred, you can tell whether the judge has heard enough. If you think he has, thank the judge for listening so patiently to you and sit down. There is now no more that you can do, and a decision will be made.

Occasionally, after you complete your last point you will notice that the judge looks perplexed. There is something still troubling him, even if he has said nothing. It is in your interest to resolve this doubt before the decision is made, in case the problem results in an unfavourable outcome for you.

The best way to resolve it is to give the judge the opportunity to say what is on his mind. Before you sit down, ask him about his concern. For example: "Before I conclude my case, is there any point that Your Honour wishes me to address further, or to address in more detail?" If the response is 'no,' thank the court and sit down. If the response is 'yes,' you are given a direct opportunity, and a final one, to clear up the judge's doubts and perhaps win your case. Take as much time and go into as much detail as you feel is necessary. You may have to restate the basis of your case, and answer questions from the judge that concern points you did not raise in reply. Don't worry about repeating yourself. If the other side objects, remind them that you are not arguing your case again, but are responding to a question from the bench that to be answered correctly requires a proper context. No doubt the judge will support you.

When you have completed your response, ask the judge if your point is clear. If it is, thank the court and sit down. If it is not, wait for the judge to ask another question and continue this process until he is satisifed that your arguments have been exhausted.

Again, you have reached the critical point. All the arguments have been heard and only the decision remains. The judge may feel that a decision can be rendered on the spot. If so, he will advise you and will proceed to deliver his judgment. Remain seated and take notes on his decision. The judge realizes that you are in court because you believe the decision that was given in the lower court was unfair. He also realizes that you have incurred expense and inconvenience to get the appeal into the court, that you have carefully prepared your case, and have presented it well. If the decision is to be given at once, the judge will want to make sure that this time it is given correctly and clearly.

The decision will often begin by a reading of the section of the statute with which you are charged. The judge will then provide a summary of the ingredients necessary to prove the case. This is usually followed by his review of the evidence, and his comments as to whether the evidence presented supports the original decision. The judge may also interpret the wording of the law under which you have been charged and apply his interpretation to the case. He may also refer to case law, that is, other cases in higher courts that have dealt with the same point you are bringing before him.

If you are arguing your own appeal the last point is probably the most difficult one to understand. Chances are that you will not be aware of other cases relevant to your own. You may even be hit with a question from the bench such as, "Is this case not really on all fours with the recent court of appeal decision?" To the judge, such a question is simple. To you, it is a mystery. What court of appeal decision? What court of appeal? This is one time when an agent or lawyer could save you. It may be, for instance, that the judge isn't all that knowledgeable about the case he remembers. An agent or lawyer can reply to his question by asking the basis of the decision, that is, the legal precedent that was set by the case, and then point out how it differs or complies with yours. Without professional help, you will have to explain that you aren't familiar with the other case, and then hope for the best.

Finally, the judge will give you the decision. He may state it right away, or he may "reserve," which means that he needs time to prepare it. Either your appeal is successful or you have lost again. If you are successful, your record will be cleared and your points will be restored. Insurance consequences will not follow, or at least they shouldn't. (If they do, switch insurance companies. You don't want to be insured by a company that finds you guilty before your guilt has been determined.)

Unsuccessful Appeals

If your appeal has not been successful, you have two choices.

You can accept the verdict of the court and take the consequences. If this means the loss of your licence or prohibitive insurance rates, so be it.

Or, you can choose to appeal again to a yet higher court of appeal, a branch of the supreme court of the province, as opposed to the provincial court. This assumes that you had a reasonable basis for questioning your original conviction, and because of the pressure of court time or because of an impatient judge dismissing your appeal out of hand, you still feel that your case has not been properly conducted or even properly heard.

This is why we have appeal courts, to correct perceived and actual miscarriages of justice in the lower courts, and to review the applications of the law. So that the system doesn't clog, however, and so that every person won't appeal just as a matter of course, the appeal courts are more jealous of their time. As a rule they do not want to hear appeals from traffic tickets. You must, therefore, earn the right to appear before them. You must tell the judge why your case deserves to have a full hearing by the court. If you can't convince him, you have no further appeal and your case is finally and irrevocably lost. If, on the other hand, you convince the judge that your case raises points which require an answer, you will be assigned a date.

But you must meet all the requirements for preparation before you will be allowed to argue your case. At this juncture, you definitely need counsel. If your case is to be heard, you will be restricted to arguing law and legal points which are beyond the lay person's ability.

To be realistic, the expense of such an appeal becomes prohibitive very quickly to all but the rich, or the poor who are eligible for legal aid. For the vast majority of Canadians, their day in court is over when they lose their first appeal. However, in the rarest of cases, a "simple" traffic ticket case can end up in the Supreme Court of Canada before nine justices, and thereby establish new law.

Checklist for Making an Appeal

This is a step-by-step summary that you can use as a checklist if you decide to appeal the verdict on your case. For a complete discussion of the appeal process, see pages 75-90.

1. Your conviction is registered at trial.
2. Study the reasons for the conviction, decide if the conviction is supportable on the evidence and make the decision whether or not to appeal.
3. Complete the procedural requirements for qualifying your appeal for the appeal court. (Check with an agent, lawyer, or court official for the correct routine to follow.)
4. Prepare your argument for the appeal, remembering that this is not a repeat of the argument made at trial.
5. Arrive early on the court date to get acquainted with the room and check the number assigned to your case on the list. Introduce yourself to the clerk as the party appealing case number "x" on the list.
6. When your case is called, introduce yourself and present your prepared argument, answering all questions from the bench fully and forthrightly.
7. Listen carefully to the arguments of the prosecution, making notes for your reply.
8. Make a brief reply argument only if necessary, and answer all questions from the bench in detail.
9. Take notes of all that is said as the decision is given.
10. If the appeal is dismissed, consider further appeal procedures based on your notes.
11. If you appeal further, consult a lawyer who will fulfill all the requirements to get the proper documents before the proper court at the proper time. The process continues until your conviction is overturned or your right of further appeal is denied.

7
The Driver as Criminal

Criminal charges can be laid in some driving offences. If this occurs, the demerit system no longer applies and the driver is charged with a criminal offence under the Criminal Code and not a ticket offence under the relevant provincial legislation. Such a charge is left to the discretion of the police officer, if he concludes that the gravity of the situation warrants it.

In Canada, the Constitution Act, 1982 (formerly the British North America Act, 1867), gives the federal government in Ottawa exclusive jurisdiction over the passing of criminal laws in Canada. These laws are found primarily in the Criminal Code. The code, as we've already noted, does include offences related to driving.

Provinces do have the right, however, to regulate vehicles on their roadways apart from criminal acts which may be committed by drivers. Each province sets speed limits, the minimum age of drivers, and determines restrictions on licences. As long as criminal consequences are not attached to such restrictions, the province is free to regulate the use of its roads. The province assesses demerit points for contravention of its rules, and may, on that basis, suspend a licence, or otherwise restrict a driver's use of the provincial roadways.

If an individual is charged with a criminal offence while driving, a conviction could result in a fine, imprisonment, or both. Demerit points are no longer an issue; your liberty is. Prosecution will be conducted in criminal courts, the same courts where people are tried for murder, theft, and other criminal offences. The prosecutor will represent the government, and the trial will proceed in much the same form as described elsewhere in this book.

The best advice that we can give our readers who may become involved in a criminal case is to get a lawyer. You are no longer known as a defendant; you are known as the accused. The consequences are far more serious, the trial process is more formal and demanding, and the work you do in preparing to defend yourself may well be inadequate.

The most familiar area of the Criminal Code involving motor vehicles is that dealing with drinking and driving. This subject is dealt with in greater detail in the section "Drinking and Driving."

Criminal Negligence in the Operation of a Motor Vehicle

The first reference to a criminal offence in the code in relation to driving is to "criminal negligence in the operation of a motor vehicle." This offence may involve either what a police officer considers dangerous driving, or what is known as failure to remain, or both. The charge will probably be referred to as criminal negligence in the operation of a motor vehicle, its technical name, but the evidence put forward will be to prove the offence of dangerous driving or of failing to remain at an accident scene. The penalty, upon conviction, can be a two-year jail term.

This should not be confused with the provincial offence of failing to remain at the scene of an accident. The provincial offence of failing to remain is very serious, as it will result in the loss of the highest number of demerit points of any provincial offence, but it will not have criminal consequences. The difference between the two charges is intent. The criminal charge involving failure to remain at the scene of an accident can be laid if the officer has reasonable grounds to suspect the driver left the scene with the intent to avoid criminal responsibility.

Consider the following example: A driver has been drinking. He starts to drive home, but on the way sideswipes a car parked on the side of the road. He stops and gets out of his car to inspect the damage and realizes that he has a very serious problem — that he is probably impaired — and as a result flees the scene. A bystander takes down the licence number of the fleeing car, calls the police, and as a result an arrest is made. The charge is criminal negligence in the operation of a motor vehicle, the evidence being that the driver failed to remain at the scene of the accident. This driver would be prosecuted in the criminal courts on the basis that he left the scene to avoid criminal prosecution, that is, to avoid prosecution on a charge of drinking and driving.

At the time of the investigation, the arresting officer has a discretion that may be critical to the fate of the motorist. It is up to the officer, as the independent agent of the crown, to assess the circumstances and decide whether leaving the scene was done with the intent to avoid criminal responsibility. Again, as in so many other cases, the reasons for your behaviour may be a decisive factor. If the reason that you left the scene was to get your very ill husband to the hospital, the fact that you may have grazed a car resulting in minor property damage would probably be a sufficient explanation to convince most police officers that your departure from the scene was not for the purpose of fleeing possible criminal responsibility. If you are given a ticket for such an accident, it is unlikely that it would be for criminal negligence.

Even in extenuating circumstances, however, you still may be technically guilty of the provincial offence of failing to remain, and demerits still may be levied against you. The provincial statutes governing the use of the roadways imposes the duty on the individual to report accidents so that

94

provincial authorities may assess the safety of the roads. Accident reports promote safety, and for this reason, among others, failure to remain carries the heaviest penalty in terms of demerit points. The investigating officer has the discretion to charge a driver with the offence of criminal negligence in the operation of a motor vehicle, or with failure to remain under the relevant provincial statute.

As in previous cases, candour may be your best friend. If the officer sees that you are trying to be helpful and truthful, you are more likely to gain the benefit of any doubt the officer may feel as to your intent, than if your attitude is adversarial.

Dangerous Driving

Dangerous driving is a charge that also involves a degree of subjectivity on the part of the investigating officer. Careless driving to one officer might be dangerous driving to another.

In some cases, the officer may not have decided which charge to lay when he starts his investigation. If you are courteous and helpful, the officer, being human, may decide that the criminal intent or reckless disregard for the consequences (the conditions necessary for a dangerous driving conviction) are lacking and the charge he lays will be the less serious charge of careless driving. It is still very serious, but it is unlikely that you will see the inside of a prison if convicted. If, on the other hand,you insult the officer, berate him or curse and carry on, he will be just as inclined to charge you with dangerous driving.

In most cases, however, the charge will clearly be one of dangerous or of careless driving. It is only in those marginal cases where behaviour at the scene will affect the charge to be laid. Most drivers will not know when their cases are marginal, and in every case, cooperation at the scene can't hurt your case.

The offence of dangerous driving is characterized by real and uncaring recklessness not found in careless driving. The motor vehicle in the hands of a dangerous driver becomes a deadly weapon. The facts in each case will determine whether the driver will be charged with dangerous driving. The courts will use terms such as "flagrant disregard for normal driving standards in the absence of a rational explanation," which means the evidence indicates that dangerous, as opposed to careless driving, is the more appropriate charge in the circumstances.

Once the charge of dangerous driving has been laid, it is most unlikely that any negotiated settlement can be reached. The case will go to the criminal courts, not the civil courts. The evidence will be presented to prove the reckless indifference of the driver to the rules of the road and the safety of others.

Playing "chicken" would be sufficient grounds for charging the motorist with dangerous driving, fleeing a police car, or racing through red lights and stop signs in total disregard for the safety of others. Alcohol need not be a part of this offence, though it often may be involved.

The essential elements in the charge of dangerous driving is *fault*. Again, if the prosecution has considerable evidence of fault, the burden shifts to the accused motorist to explain and answer the charge. If you speed through a red light and hit another car which was plainly visible, for example, the facts indicate a charge of dangerous driving is warranted, as you were obviously not watching the road. You would, in this case, have to convince the court that what was involved was not an instance of dangerous driving, but was rather a series of events that can be defined as inadvertent negligence, or possibly as a momentary lapse. Maybe a bee landed on your cheek, and in trying to wave it away your attention was distracted and you pushed the accelerator down by mistake. Or it could be the case that your passenger had a heart attack and fell across you, caused the car to accelerate through a stop sign and resulted in injuries requiring hospital care. If you have been taken from the scene and cannot explain the circumstances, the officer could arrive, observe the chaos, and conclude that dangerous driving was the cause.

It is obvious that the facts of each case become very important. It can be argued that in a situation such as the first, the motorist did not have the intention to commit the criminal act of dangerous driving, but was rather the unfortunate victim of a set of unusual, uncontrollable circumstances. In such a case the charge of dangerous driving may not be sustained.

However, before the entire population shows up in court with evidence as to the migratory habits of bees, it is important to remember the context in which the explanation is presented. No court will believe a bee story when a five mile chase is involved. The explanation offered as a defence must, of course, be true, and being true, must also be a logical and reasonable answer to the details of the charge as read in court.

Drinking and Driving

Alcohol and its Consequences

A new trend is emerging in the Canadian courts. They are becoming much more severe with drivers accused of alcohol-related driving offences. Instructions have been sent by the attorneys-general of the provinces to jail offenders, when formerly mere fines and licence suspensions were considered sufficient punishment. The days of the "slap on the wrist" are over. Society as a whole is reacting against what is seen as needless carnage on the road. Society is recognizing that the partnership of alcohol and driving is a deadly one.

As in the case of dangerous driving, the most obvious consequence of a drinking-related offence is jail. In the past,

97

this penalty was usually reserved for the repeat offender, but this is not necessarily the case today. Depending on the facts and the damage done, a first offender may find himself behind bars.

Another major consequence is civil liability. The crown, through the investigating police officer, will charge the offender under the Criminal Code, but if the drinking driver has caused injury to people or property, the injured persons or the owners of the damaged property also have the opportunity to sue the drunk driver in the civil courts for damages.

Insurance then, becomes a major issue in this case, though it may be trivial compared to the other damages involved. If your insurance company becomes involved, they may be liable to the extent of your policy coverage with them. If a driver's policy limit is two hundred thousand dollars, for example, and as a result of driving while impaired he permanently cripples a young person to whom the court awards five hundred thousand dollars, in damages, the consequences become staggering. Aside from the tragic implications of an accident such as this, the driver's future premiums are going to rise dramatically.

The best advice is don't drive if you intend to drink. Similarly, if you have guests who have been drinking, as the host or hostess begin to cut down on their drinks several hours before they drive home, cut their supply off completely, or insist they take a cab.

Drinking affects individuals differently. We are all familiar with the legendary person who can drink all night, party to the hilt, drive home without feeling any effect whatever, and get up bright and early the next morning. On the other hand, we all know of the normally sedate individual who becomes an extroverted, aggressive bear after one drink. Every party seems to have its happy drinker, its giddy drinker, its aggressive drinker, its obnoxious drinker, and its tiresome drinker.

The only common denominator among them is their alcoholic consumption. It would take a scientist to discuss how alcohol, a poison, is absorbed by the body into the blood stream and broken down over time. The metabolic process varies with each person. The only constant is that no one is immune. The legendary drinker as well as the novice is affected, however apparently competent they remain.

Nothing is more tragic than the news that a person has killed or been killed while impaired behind the wheel of a car. Because alcohol seems such an integral part of society, because the government depends on its sale for revenue and television tells us we cannot be happy or complete without it, the tragic results of drinking and driving have in the past been considered sad but inevitable.

In the last few years, that has been changing. The great Canadian pastime of drinking and driving is past its prime. Mothers Against Drunken Driving (MADD) and others have been lobbying for stronger penalties for offenders. They have been monitoring court proceedings and reporting on what they have felt were inadequate attitudes in regard to sentencing. They have petitioned the provinces to enforce the laws more vigorously, and petitioned Ottawa for tougher legislation.

In December 1984, the Honourable John Crosbie, QC, MP, then Minister of Justice, introduced legislation in the House of Commons that would, if enacted, result in tougher attitudes being taken to drinking and driving. Police departments are being encouraged to conduct roadside testing and in Vancouver this effort brought the new no nonsense attitude home, when thousands of drivers were stopped at random and their state of sobriety checked. In Toronto, the Police Department several years ago, in the west end of the city, started a similar program called RIDE (Reduce Impaired Driving in Etobicoke). Despite the initial cry from civil libertarians about their rights being infringed in having to prove their cars were safe and they were sober, the program has been hailed as a great success and has been adopted throughout Ontario and across the country.

A positive sign of the changing times is the new attitude of healthy living which seems to be emerging. Breweries and distilleries see their sales stagnating and actually declining. It is no longer socially acceptable to become blind drunk at a party and then embark on the great adventure of driving home. This development holds most hope for the future.

The Criminal Code deals extensively with the area of drinking and driving. The sections are complex, and have been interpreted in even more complex ways by judges dealing with the code and what it means in particular cases.

Some of the possibilities defy logic. How many people would guess that they can be charged with the offence of "driving while their ability is impaired" (to use the words of the section) when the car is not moving and they are sitting in the back seat? As strange and illogical as it sounds, it is a criminal offence. Say a driver and another person drive to a park with a case of beer. They get out of the car and drink the beer. They then decide to watch the moon come up from the back seat. An officer comes along and sees a beer bottle being thrown out the window. As he questions them he notices the unmistakable odour of beer on their breath. Upon further investigation, the officer determines that the driver's ability is impaired. Even though seated in the back seat of a stopped car, the driver has the care and control of the car, and the charge could be laid. Imagine his surprise when the driver realizes the penalty could be up to two thousand dollars and imprisonment for six months for this first offence. The offence in this section is not that the accused is driving while in an alcoholic fog, but that his ability to drive is hindered by alcohol, whether driving or not.

It is also important to remember that while alcohol is the major drug the section of the code is meant to combat, it also covers any other drug. If, for example, the revellers above had decided that instead of beer they preferred to smoke a little hashish or to temper their hashish with a little beer, the charge is still valid. Medications are also covered here. For example: A woman with a heart problem has been socially drinking at a class reunion, though carefully monitoring the number of drinks she has. Leaving the party, she remembers that it is past time for her medication. She swallows one of the pills her doctor has prescribed, and starts to drive home. Though unaware of the fact, she may be impaired with the combination of her prescribed drug and her intake of alcohol. If she were stopped in a spot check she could be charged for impaired driving.

In this case, it is not a defence that the driver did not appreciate that her condition was impaired. She knew that she was consuming a drug, and she consumed the alcohol of her own free will. Along the same lines, it is no defence if one is too drunk to appreciate that an offence is being committed.

Similarly, suppose George goes out with the boys for a night at his favourite suburban bar. About midnight, George reaches for his wallet to buy his round for the boys and drops the change he is intending to use as a tip. When he bends over, he realizes that he can't seem to get his fingers to pick up the coins. Several of his buddies think this is quite amusing, and so does George. In fact, he finds it so amusing he can't stop laughing.

However, George suddenly realizes that the premises will soon close and his car is his only way home, as public transportation has closed down. George realizes he is probably impaired, so he finishes the round he has just purchased and then orders a coffee to sober himself up for the drive home. It is no defence that George thinks all is well because he has had a cup of coffee. George is impaired, and will still be impaired by the time he tries to drive home. No one forced him to drink all those rounds and coffee is medically no help, and no defence.

Road-Side Testing

The scene is by now familiar to most Canadian drivers. You come around a corner at night and observe the flashing lights of a police car at the side of the road. At about the same time your headlights illuminate the reflector bands on the officer's uniform at the side of the road. With flashlight in hand, he signals to you to pull your car over to the side of the road. He comes over to the side of your car and politely requests you to produce your driver's licence, your insurance, and the car's ownership. He also asks you to demonstrate your high beams, your turn signals, your brakes, and your backing lights. If he detects an odour of an alcoholic beverage on your breath, suspects that you may have been drinking, or suspects you have been using drugs that might impair your ability to drive a car, he asks you some more questions and may request you to get out of your car. If you show reluctance, he may advise you that if you do not comply you face the possibility of being charged with obstructing police in the performance of their duties.

If you appear unsteady on your feet, or in any way incoherent or unresponsive, you may be asked to walk a line, touch your fingers to your nose, or other tests that permit the officer to assess your alertness.

There is a popular misconception that you are only stopped for drunk driving if you are weaving all over the road. There are, however, numerous other circumstances — a headlight burned out or a routine check — that might bring you to the attention of an officer. In such a case it may be wise not to volunteer too much information, and to warn one's companions to exercise the same discretion.

A case in point involves a typical investigation of a speeding infraction. An officer was on a radar assignment and had recorded a speed for a car sufficient to justify a ticket. He signalled the driver to pull over and requested him to produce his driver's licence, insurance, and proof of ownership.

The driver, as usual, asked the officer why he had been stopped. The officer told him that he had been speeding.

His reaction was typical; he denied that he had been speeding. The officer said no, he had indeed been speeding and that the radar had recorded a speed considerably in excess of the limit.

At this point, the driver's wife, who had been quietly observing the incident from the passenger seat, decided to intervene in an attempt to rescue the situation. She leaned over so that she could see the investigating officer through the open window and said:

"He's right officer. He couldn't have been speeding. I never let him speed when he's been drinking." His wife was, unfortunately, right about at least one of the two statements; he had been drinking, and was subsequently charged with impaired driving.

In all provinces except British Columbia and Quebec, roadside testing, that is, breath analysis, of a motorist is permitted if an officer has a reasonable suspicion that the motorist is driving with alcohol in his body. The officer can order the motorist to provide a breath sample either on the scene, or another place where testing facilities are available.

Several years ago, the Metropolitan Toronto Police Department, as part of its annual Christmas blitz to reduce impaired driving, began setting up road-side testing facilities and ordering suspected drivers to submit to these tests. The legal issue arose as to what right the police had to order people to submit to this process, which was, in effect, leading to a potential criminal charge.

Under the provisions of the Ontario Highway Traffic Act (the statute governing the conduct of motorists on the road) at the time, the mandate of the police was to enforce the laws of the road. But the questions were: Did a motorist have to stop? And when stopped, did he have to submit to testing? As a result, a road-side testing section was added to the Criminal Code, and the Highway Traffic Act was amended so that an officer could order any driver to stop at any time for any reason. This made it an offence to disregard such a direction. In light of this provision, the motorist is stuck. He has to stop, and, if requested, has to submit to the test.

Breath Samples

The Criminal Code allows an officer to request a sample of your breath if he thinks alcohol (and in this case alcohol only) has been consumed within the preceding two hours, and he believes that the present ability of the motorist is impaired. He may also request a sample if he suspects that the proportion of alcohol in the driver's blood exceeds eighty milligrams of alcohol in one hundred millilitres of blood (the legal proof of impairment).

If the officer demands a breath sample, he must use one of three approved devices as set out in the Criminal Code. It would, therefore, be in order to ask the officer for the name of the device used. If the device is not one of the three, the test may well be invalid. Write down the name of the device, or ask the officer to write it down for you. If you ask politely, this is not an unreasonable request. If it is refused, get the officer's number and subsequently you can get the information from the officer's superior.

It is a very difficult part of the Criminal Code to contest. All the officer has to do is tell the court that he had a reasonable suspicion that a driver had alcohol in his body. If the court decides that his opinion was formed in good faith, the driver will not be able to contest it.

Back in the 1960s, Sonny Liston, the former world heavyweight boxing champ, was pulled over on an American street and, as the officer believed he smelled alcohol on his breath, he was charged with a drinking and driving offence. Liston replied that he had not been consuming alcohol, but that the odour on his breath was caused by his copious consumption of carrot juice. Being a professional boxer, he needed the vitamin A found in carrot juice to maintain his excellent vision. The officer listened to this reasonable excuse and arrested him anyway. Before the carrot juice tin becomes commonplace in Canadian vehicles, the motorist should be prepared to walk the line or perform some other test to objectively prove sobriety before refusing a breath test on the grounds the officer has no reasonable grounds to demand a sample.

Issue has been taken on occasion with the reliability of breath samples as indicators of intoxication. There is also some dispute that the limit set by law (eighty milligrams of alcohol in one hundred millilitres of blood) actually indicates impairment or intoxication. Medically, it may be a good argument. The legendary drinker could drink all night and not be impaired in the sense of being unable to function. Conversely, the amateur may have one drink and become totally incoherent. The law, however, must apply some standard, even though it may convict the functioning legendary drinker and acquit the hopelessly impaired amateur. Blood samples give the same results — the technology of breathalyzer machines is now quite sophisticated — and we still face the human problem of individual variation. The maintenance of the testing machine, however, may not always be up to the same high standards, and this may be a question to raise in your defence.

The police are given the widest possible discretion here, in the interest of protecting the public. And a refusal to provide a breath sample or to accompany the officer in order to provide one, is an offence, with a maximum penalty of two thousand dollars and six months in jail.

His demand can be made at any time after the driver is pulled over. Unlike the cautioning which is given to an accused, the demand needn't be made in any particular form, as long as it's clear that the sample is required. Obviously in some cases the officer may not know right away if he's going to demand a sample, so the motorist must stay in his presence until the investigation is complete.

When the Bill of Rights was passed by parliament in 1960 these sections of the Criminal Code were challenged and held to be valid. It is unlikely that the Charter of Rights and Freedoms will affect a change in the Criminal Code because it is recognized that these provisions promote a social good, namely, reducing drunk driving. At the moment, however, early decisions are going both ways. The final word on the subject will come from the Supreme Court of Canada.

Some people will refuse on the grounds that they have to talk to their lawyer before deciding whether or not they must give a sample. It is a reasonable request, but if you try to contact your lawyer but can't (through no fault of the police) within a reasonable time, you have to give a sample anyway.

This is not a lawyer's finest hour, incidentally. The phone rings at 3:00 A.M. and the lawyer, who has worked until midnight preparing a jury address for the next morning, has to get dressed, drive fifty miles to the police station and probably tell his client that he has no excuse to refuse the test. His client wouldn't take this advice, because it is such an important matter, over the phone.

Even if a lawyer is on his way, the police may become tired of waiting, and charge the driver with a refusal. They may need the evidence right away for a conviction, as time will break down the alcohol in the blood. So the test has to be taken within two hours of the time of detainment.

Even if the driver says that his lawyer has advised him against taking the test, it may not help. He can still be charged with refusal, and the lawyer could be in trouble as well for advising his client to commit a criminal offence.

It is our experience that people at the scene do not always behave rationally. Some are so convinced of the state of their sobriety that a mere breath sample is not sufficient. They are determined to walk the line, count backwards, and conjugate verbs. Some will insist that the breath sample is not proof enough and will insist that in the best interests of justice a sample of their blood should be taken for analysis. In the latter case, however, if it means refusing the breath sample — the method that the judicial system uses to evaluate impairment — the offer could be used as evidence of the driver's refusal to take the test.

If you are stopped on suspicion of drunk driving, the best advice is not to argue with the officer. If you have been drinking at all, you can't depend on your judgment, and the last thing you need is an even more complicated, unpleasant situation. If you are indeed impaired you've already acted foolishly. The consequences can be very grave, so request at your earliest opportunity to see a lawyer. Insist on this right preferably before you submit to the test. You should be able to call your lawyer and consult with him at the police station before you give a sample. You should never refuse outright, but if the officers push for a test on the scene, tell them that you prefer to discuss the case with your lawyer before you submit to the test, and suggest the test be given at the station after he has advised you. This will give you time to collect your thoughts, and consider, with the advice of your lawyer, what is to be done.

Reasonable Excuses to Refuse

The only allowance made for refusing to give a breath sample is a *reasonable* excuse. Police officers, and subsequently the courts, hear hundreds of excuses, and a few of them have been allowed as reasonable. If a motorist is not allowed to confer with a lawyer in private, it has been decided that this amounts to a denial of the right to counsel. In that context, the courts have decided you have a reasonable excuse to refuse. In another instance, an out-of-province visitor was unable to reach her lawyer because she was not allowed to make a long distance call from the police station. The court decided in her favour and the case was dismissed.

Perhaps the most obvious case of a reasonable excuse, is

when the driver is unable to understand the demand. If the person is so drunk that he is barely conscious, it would be pushing the case to charge him with refusing to provide a sample. It has been done, but the court has been obliged to dismiss the charges. The accused might be guilty of numerous offences, the least of which is public intoxication, but he is not guilty of refusing to provide a breath sample upon demand.

Another example of a reasonable excuse that might be accepted by the court, is if a person honestly believes that the machine is not working properly. If the motorist has been sitting watching others being tested and has noticed that the results are widely erratic or has noticed that even a breeze from an opened door sets off a reading on the machine, the test should be refused on that ground. The court must be convinced, however, that the defendant had an *objective* reason for refusing, not just a belief that "all those machines are rigged." If the driver asked the officer to open the door, for example, and see how the machine was affected, and the officer did in fact see the problem for himself, that would be objective evidence.

What is acceptable as a reasonable excuse will depend on the facts of each case. If the nearest test facility is one hundred miles away and the driver is going to be stranded there, it might be considered reasonable to refuse. That will not necessarily close the issue, though. If the officer is determined to arrest you, he can lay another alcohol-related charge.

In any event, if you are going to refuse to provide a sample of your breath when it is demanded by a police officer, you should realize that in most cases, there is no reasonable excuse. You will most likely be compounding the problem which resulted in the demand being made in the first place.

Over Eighty Milligrams

Alcohol acts upon every individual differently, but at some

point everyone's ability to drive safely is affected. The law has arbitrarily set eighty milligrams of alcohol in one hundred millilitres of blood as the legal limit for unimpaired driving. This means that exceeding this limit is illegal, whether or not your ability to drive has actualy been impaired.

This standard puts the experienced social drinker, who prides himself on his ability to hold his alcohol without appearing drunk, on notice that the mere accumulation of alcohol in the blood is sufficient to carry criminal consequences. There are all sorts of rule-of-thumb calculations on how much a person can drink and still drive legally, such as one drink per hour, or one and a half beers per hour. Whether these are true or not would, of course, depend on the size of the person, the volume of blood in his body, and the strength of the drinks.

We can't stress too much that the reading itself of over eighty milligrams is sufficient to prove guilt. That you had no intention to commit the offence, or did not realize you had that much to drink is no defence. The reading alone proves your guilt.

Breath sample evidence is very difficult to fight in court. Either it indicates that the offence has been committed or it does not. Except for the possibilities discussed below, the chances of being found not guilty are remote.

Defences

If you are a driver faced with an alcohol or drug-related traffic offence, it is essential to get a lawyer. First of all, your liberty is at issue and the courts will be only too willing to jail you. Secondly, a conviction is guaranteed to send your insurance rates through the roof. Thirdly, a conviction means you have a criminal record. This means, among other things, that on any job application you will have to list this record. In today's particularly tight job market a criminal record is a complication no one can afford.

Your first line of defence is the ticket itself, outlining the charge. In the criminal sphere, it is known as the "information." Even more so than in a ticket for a civil offence, this information must be correct. In all cases, the accused must be properly named. The date and place of the offence must be outlined clearly. There must be no room for doubt in the mind of the accused about the charge that has to be met. The section of the Criminal Code under which the accused is charged must be complete and correct. Amendments to the ticket in court will be much more difficult for the prosecution to obtain.

The reason for this is obvious. The accused must have every chance to mount a proper defence. If the section of the Criminal Code is not present, if it is mistaken, it can confuse and disorient the defendant. The entire criminal process is difficult and confusing enough; there is no room to further compound the problem by failing to properly inform him of the exact charge. Some people may argue that such quibbles are mere technicalities. In one sense, that may be true. But the resources of the individual are far fewer than those of the court, and it is only fair that the state should prove its case properly, when the consequences for the accused will be so severe.

Before you make a decision as to how to plead, review the information before you. Ask yourself the following questions:

Is the information complete in its description of the offence committed?
Is the information clear and unambiguous?
Are all the necessary elements of the offence included, such as time, place, date, and section of the Criminal Code?
Is the section of the Criminal Code under which you are charged stated correctly, and does it correspond with the verbal and written information you have been given?

Obviously, this type of review can best be performed by a lawyer or an agent with the appropriate experience. As in the case of civil offences some mistakes on the ticket are correctable by the court, if the prosecution requests it, and some are not. As we stated earlier, it is beyond the scope of this book to attempt to classify which mistakes can be corrected and those which cannot. The important thing is to realize that the prosecution must prove its case beyond a reasonable doubt. And the first opportunity to raise a doubt in the mind of a judge, is to indicate sloppy work by the police and prosecution in the preparation of the documents on which their case rests.

The actual introduction of evidence is no different than in a civil case. Witnesses are examined and cross-examined, and documents are filed for the record of the court. The great difference lies in the "burden of proof." As mentioned earlier, in a criminal charge you must be guilty beyond a reasonable doubt.

Here are a few points that you and your lawyer may want to consider if you end up in court on a drinking-related charge. If the prosecution wishes to introduce documentary evidence, such as certificates of analysts, make sure that the forms are filled out properly and signed, if necessary, by persons with the proper qualifications. If readings were taken on machines, and are to be entered as evidence, make sure that the machine is authorized and that it has been tested by a qualified person. Be sure that times have been recorded throughout, especially if you think an unreasonable delay may have occurred at some point in the investigation. This may be difficult, as alcohol or drugs are known to distort one's appreciation of the passing of time. Again, in this regard, knowledge of police procedure is of some help. The officer's notes will help the prosecution establish what happened at what time. The only problem is that often these notes are not written at the time of the incident, but rather at the officer's first convenience and if that involves a lengthy period of time their accuracy may be questionable. These notes can also help determine if any demands that were required to be made were made clearly. A muddled mind may not have been able to understand what was being asked. The accuracy of the officer's notes and knowledge of police routine may be helpful in your defence.

Curative Treatment

In certain provinces, there is an alternative available with regard to the sentencing of drinking and driving offenders. When the defendant pleads guilty or is found guilty, the court may order a conditional or absolute discharge of the driver through a probation order, on the condition that the motorist attends a treatment program for alcohol or drug dependence. The driver must follow through with the program, however, and the sentence cannot be "contrary to the public interest."

But many prosecutors are now arguing that "public interest" demands jail for those who combine driving with alcohol or drugs. The trend towards tougher sentences has been noticeable in the last few years. So even in provinces where such curative treatment is available, it may become more difficult to argue that such treatment, rather than jail, is in the public interest.

It should be noted, however, that public interest can change from one day to the next. A few years ago, in anticipation of the visit of the Queen Mother to Toronto, the local police went on a blitz to clear the streets of the usual characters so familiar in the downtown area. For a two-day period, not a "wino" was to be seen. They had all been arrested, presumably in the public interest, for being drunk or for having alcohol in a public place. The day after the Queen Mother left, they were all back on the streets. Actually, very few Torontonians even noticed that they'd ever been gone!

112

8
The Future

The Impaired Driver and the Future

Changes are coming in the way that society deals with the problem of the drinking or drugged driver. It used to be assumed that the offences relating to impairment dealt with the inevitable results of Saturday night at the local. However, in recent years, it has become obvious that the impaired driver can be impaired from drugs as readily as from alcohol. It is becoming a matter of concern that some cross-country truckers are rolling down the highways stoned on amphetamines to keep them awake.

The carnage on the roads has finally taken its toll. Where first-time offenders were once given fines for impaired driving, many are now facing jail sentences, and the public overwhelmingly supports this crackdown. Tough laws are in force in other countries and the pressure is growing in Canada to implement similar provisions here.

As outlined in the earlier section on alcohol-related offences, the problem of the prosecution often has been to detect and prove the offence. This is why the breathalyzer provisions were first introduced into the Criminal Code. Even tougher legislation is being considered which will make prosecuting offenders easier. Whether this legislation infringes unnecessarily on the rights of the individual, under common law or the Charter of Rights, will be an active issue before the courts in the coming years.

A study recently found that in Ontario, 26 percent of fatally-injured drivers had drugs in their bodies other than alcohol. In another study done in Texas, blood samples from persons arrested for "driving under the influence," where breathalyzer results did not indicate impairement, detected drugs in 72 percent of the blood samples analyzed. These results and other studies have been summarized in a report of the Law Reform Commission of Canada on driving offences relating to alcohol and drugs.

Future Legislation

The present provisions of the Criminal Code in relation to drinking offences and driving are inadequate when the suspected driver is found in an unconscious state or when he has suffered some injury to his mouth that prevents effective use of a breathalyzer. The driver's impairment could be established from the analysis of his blood or urine, but a provision in the Criminal Code states that no one is required to give such a sample, and if such a sample is obtained without the person's informed agreement, those taking it could be found guilty of assault. Drug-related driving offences are even more difficult, as the breathalyzer can't detect drugs. The result is that the prosecution can know that an offence has been committed, and still be unable to prove it.

Some suggestions have been made on what the best method of dealing with this problem might be. Forced blood samples are one option that may soon be acted upon, especially with the election of a Progressive Conservative government, which ran on a strong law-and-order platform.

Blood and Urine Testing

In some jurisdictions, such as the United Kingdom, the State of Victoria in Australia, New Zealand, and in Canada in British Columbia and Manitoba, statutes similar to that described above have been passed. They have covered the common law problem of assault by making it lawful to obtain these samples. The more difficult problem of the reliability of the results from the sampling process has been solved by improving the analysis methods.

It is easy enough with current-day science to make an accurate determination of the amount of alcohol or other drugs in the body from a sample of blood or urine. Where a problem may arise is in the time factor. Is it reasonable to assume that in most cases by the time the blood sample is taken it will show less of an alcohol or drug concentration than at the time the person was stopped? This is true in the case of a blood sample test for alcohol, because blood breaks down and dilutes alcohol over time, but is more difficult to say about other drugs, as these are unpredictable and largely unresearched. But logically one would expect it to be true. Urine tests are less predictable yardsticks. More variables enter in, such as how full the bladder was when drugs or alcohol were consumed, and how long it has been since the bladder was last emptied.

At present, the definition of impairment in relation to drugs is uncertain. If eighty milligrams of alcohol in one hundred millilitres of blood is the legal definition of impairment, how many parts of THC (the operative component in marijuana) in how many parts of blood might produce a comparable effect? Especially since, in fact, the mere presence of eighty milligrams may not even mean the person is impaired. It may only mean that they are guilty of the offence of having that proportion of alcohol in the blood. Similarly, how does one decide how much of a certain drug will cause impairment? And what about drugs used in combination with alcohol or with other drugs? It is obvious that these decisions are complex and will be constantly subject to revision as new drugs appear within the general population and further studies offer clearer definitions of impairment. It is possible that what may not be an offence one day could become one by the next.

One way that the law has addressed this type of problem in the past is by allowing "presumption." If a sample of your blood indicates that you have ingested an illegal drug, a "presumption" is allowed that you are impaired. If legislation were passed to this effect it would eliminate the prosecution's problem of defining drug impairment with regard to illegal drugs. It does not address legal drugs, however, and the problem of defining impairment for prescription drugs would still exist. Codeine, for example, can produce impairment, but is frequently included in prescribed cough remedies.

Drug classification will, without doubt, give problems to lawmakers in years to come. There is no simple solution in a society that uses as many chemicals as ours, both legal and illegal.

Penalties

If parliament plans to confront the problem of drug-induced impaired driving, it will be necessary to provide appropriate enforcement. The Criminal Code already provides that it is an offence to refuse a reasonable demand for a breath sample. It would seem logical that the same kind of provision might be added to the Criminal Code when a blood or urine sample is refused.

Again, it may be found that there are legitimate reasons for refusing to provide such a sample upon request, but inevitably the onus will be on the accused to prove that his excuse qualifies as "reasonable." Otherwise, the law would have no particular effect.

Another method of enforcement that is allowed in New Zealand is to submit the defendant's refusal into evidence in the form of an "adverse finding." This would allow the court to infer that the accused was, by refusing, admitting guilt. This is similar to the breathalyzer provisions, where refusal is an offence comparable to that of the charge it would prove.

A more problematic solution which has been suggested, although it might create as many difficulties as it would solve, would be to allow the police to use reasonable force to get a sample. This is, of course, not permitted right now, but reasonable force is allowable in certain cases; for example, when the police want a suspect's fingerprints.

The problem of the use of force is obvious in any case. If the accused is unwilling to submit to the procedure it is hard to see how reasonable force could be applied in order to obtain a urine sample. It is not so absurd when it comes to obtaining a sample of blood, but is, however, a course of action that raises a number of concerns, not the least of which is the potential for serious medical complications.

Suppose an officer arrives on the scene to find the accused unconscious and, upon investigation, decides that a blood sample is necessary. How would it be determined whether or not his decision was reasonable? In the unconscious state, consent is not an issue — but medical considerations may be. In any case, it would be necessary to get a medical opinion on whether the sample could be safely taken. And when the interests of the investigating officer and the attending doctor differ, medical considerations must come first. Suppose a blood sample cannot be obtained reasonably? Should the police then be permitted to take a urine sample? In most cases, we would hope not. However, the legislature may decide that in certain cases this could be allowed. These are issues that time and the courts will resolve.

Recently, in Prince Edward Island, an officer was at the hospital after an accident when one of the victims who was unconscious, was being treated. The attending physician gave the officer a sample of the patient's blood, which was then analyzed. These results were later presented in court. The court, in very strong language, rejected any such use of the blood or its analysis. The judge was extremely critical of the doctor and the police officer, who had taken the blood without authority or permission.

Although legislation may sometime in the future permit such samples to be taken and used, it is clear from this decision that without specific legislation such use will not be tolerated. It is certain to be an interesting issue in the coming months and years.

The Charter of Rights and Freedoms

The Charter of Rights and Freedoms is the name attached to the first sections of the document now known as The Constitution Act, 1982. It immediately became a media event, and has found itself cited in many diverse areas of legal argument ever since it was enacted. The charter is framed in generally vague terms, and the problem with such wording is that definition must be given to them before they can be applied to the circumstances of a particular case.

The process of interpreting of a document like the Charter of Rights can be both exciting and disconcerting. In certain areas, it is difficult to see how the document can even be cited in all conscience. It is possible to cite the provisions of the charter in virtually any set of circumstances, but in doing so we run the danger of trivializing the document. On the other hand, the general wording of the document means that it can evolve to comply with the social circumstances of the day.

The evolution of such a document is an interesting study. Although the men who composed the United States Constitution could never have foreseen that the U.S. would evolve into the industrial giant of today, the U.S. is still able to use the ideas and principles laid out in that document. Through amendments (which are legislated), and interpretation, the document of 1789 is still as valid today as it was at its drafting.

The Constitution Act, 1982, has already been amended. It is evident that the same process of amendment that has applied to the American constitution will occur in Canada. By contrast, the United Kingdom has no written constitution, but has somehow managed to cope since the Battle of Hastings without one. There, the common law has evolved as the protection of the citizen against the arbitrary use of power by the Crown. Canada has both the common law and now The Constitution Act, 1982. Possibly this perceived need arose out of qualms of conscience arising from the imposition of the War Measures Act in the October crisis of 1970. Probably we will never know.

The advent of the charter has found it being used as a vehicle to promote all forms of causes. Lawyers are already testing the limits of the loose language used. Recently, it was argued in the appeal courts in Toronto that the Charter of Rights guaranteed that women could dance nude in bars, despite both the Criminal Code provisions against nudity in a public place and the municipal by-laws of the Metropolitan Toronto government. The argument was made that the by-laws deprived the performers of the right, as guaranteed in the charter, of freedom of expression. Counsel for Metro Toronto argued that, among other things, this type of activity was not what parliament had in mind when passing the charter, and to accede to this argument would be to trivialize an otherwise noble document.

The charter has been referred to in many ways, but the best description is probably as a living tree with its roots deep in the experience of Canada. Nevertheless, the charter will have to adopt its general principles to specific situations as they arise in the cases before the courts.

One area that a charter argument may be made is in the area of the taking of a blood sample from an individual by a doctor under instructions from a police officer acting in the course of his duty, if such a provision should be adopted as an amendment to the Criminal Code. Section 8 of The Constitution Act provides that a citizen of Canada should be secure against any unreasonable search or seizure. Adoption of such an amendment to the code would raise the question as to whether our hypothetical unconscious motorist had been, in fact, subjected to an unreasonable search or possibly seizure, if his blood were taken. On the application of common sense, it would seem that a lack of consent would indicate that such a course of action was unreasonable, and therefore should not be permitted as being contrary to the provisions of the charter.

First appearances, however, may be deceiving. The charter must be looked at as a whole, and each section read with an eye to every other section and the provisions contained in those other sections. The taking of blood from the hypothetical unconscious motorist may in fact be legitimate under another section of the charter, providing for reasonable limits being placed on the rights of an individual that can be clearly justified in a free and democratic society. Is it a proper limitation upon the freedom of an individual to allow blood to be taken from a person without consent, compatible with the traditions and practices of a free and democratic society?

Charter arguments are going to be long, complex and varied. They will frequently depart from traditional legal argument involving the study of the words of statutes and case law. In a charter argument, it is not beyond the realm of possibility that, in our blood sample case, the courts would be asked to look at the words of the Criminal Code amendments, the words of the charter, and the Canadian experience, in relation to similar testing through the cases on breathalyzers, and the reasonable excuse cases that underline what types of restrictions and exceptions the law provides.

When you start to argue what is or is not compatible with the interests of a free and democratic society, the argument leaves the strictly "legal" realm. Such an argument might show, for example, what other countries as free and democratic as Canada have found to be reasonable limitations on the individual. As well, it is likely that studies which have been done on the effectiveness of more stringent provisions against impaired drivers will be introduced as evidence to the court of how laws can help promote safer roads to the benefit of society.

In opposition, however, one would argue that the common law position is that the procedure is an assault. From there it could then be argued that in accordance with the charter, the individual has the right to liberty and security of the person and the right not to be deprived of such *except* in accordance with the principles of fundamental justice. Arguments would then be made as to what constitutes fundamental justice.

It can quickly be seen that judges will soon find themselves on new and slippery ground when presented with cases that include charter arguments. Not only must they be able to follow the traditional legal arguments, but now they must digest and respond intelligently to arguments based as much on philosophy, political science, sociology, and history as they are on law.

Index

of, 92; defences to, 109–111
Crosbie, Hon. John, Q.C., M.P., 99
Curative treatment (drinking),
112

Dangerous driving, 95–97; vs.
careless driving, 95; and fault,
96
Demerit points, 18–20; consequences of, 19; listing of, 20.
See also Reciprocity
Documents, filing before the
court, 46
Doppler, Christian Johann, 28
Dress (before the court), *See*
Court: dressing for
Drinking and driving, 97–112;
civil liability for, 98; insurance
consequences, 98; road-side
testing, 102; over 80 milligrams, 108–09. *See also* Breath
samples; Criminal offences;
Curative treatment

Evidence, rules of, 12

Guilty, plea of, 7; consequences
of, 8; with an explanation,
7–9

Impaired Driver: blood and
urine testing, 114–16; proposed penalties, 116–18. *See
also* Charter of Rights and
Freedoms; Criminal offences;
Drinking and driving
Insurance, 21–24; and criminal
conviction, 22; and traffic
convictions, 22, 23
Interpreters, 40

Judge, addressing of, 44
Justice of the Peace, addressing
of, 44

Koran, The, 55

Lawyers, 35

Mobile digital radar (MDR). *See*
Speeding
Motion for dismissal, 48–51;
when made, 49; grounds
for, 49

Not guilty, 10–11; choosing a
plea of, 9; consequences of
plea, 10

Peremptory court date, 38
Plea bargaining. *See* Pre-trial
agreed conclusion
Pleas. *See* Guilty; Not guilty
Pointts Limited, 36
Police officer: as an agent of
crown, 1; discretion of, 95,
105; power to stop vehicles,
1; power to demand breath
sample, 104–07
Pre-trial agreed conclusion,
negotiating of, 39–40
Procedure at the scene, 16–17;
courtesy, 2. *See also* Accident
reports; Traffic tickets
Prosecution adjournments, 38
Prosecutor, 43–44
Provincial Offences Traffic
Court. *See* Court

Radar. *See* Speeding
Reciprocity, 24